O'BRIEN POCKET HISTORY OF

IRISH WRITERS

FROM SWIFT TO HEANEY

A concise guide to the extraordinary canon of Irish writing

An informative guide to the great and the lesser-known names in Irish writing in the English language, in chronological order and with themes, with concise and interesting commentary from one of the leading experts in the area. Gives a complete overview that will be useful to both general reader and scholar.

A. NORMAN JEFFARES has written on and edited the work of many Irish writers, including Swift, Farquhar, Goldsmith, Edgeworth, George Moore, James Joyce. He is particularly known for his books on W B Yeats. He lectured at Trinity College, Dublin, and at the universities of Groningen and Edinburgh, and held chairs at Adelaide, Leeds and Stirling.

ACKNOWLEDGEMENTS

PHOTOGRAPHS and ILLUSTRATIONS
The publishers wish to thank the following for permission to reproduce illustrations and photographs: Robert Allen Photography for Jonathan Swift; Michael K Barron for Brian Friel; Colm Henry for Seamus Heaney; John O'Brien for Kate O'Brien; all others original paintings by Thomas Spelman, taken from reproductions by the Oisín Gallery, Dublin.

Austin Clarke, 'The Straying Student' by kind permission of R Dardis Clarke, 21 Pleasants Street, Dublin 8; Douglas Hyde, translation of 'For thee I shall not die' by kind permission of Douglas Sealy; Oliver St John Gogarty, 'Ringsend' by kind permission Oliver D Gogarty SC; John Hewitt, 'The Glens' by kind permission of copyright holder and Blackstaff Press; Louis MacNeice, extract by kind permission of Faber & Faber from Autumn Journal; W R Rodgers, 'The Net' by kind permission of the author and The Gallery Press from Poems (1993); Yeats, The Wanderings of Oisin, from The Collected Poems of W B Yeats by kind permission of AP Watt Ltd on behalf of Michael Yeats.

O'BRIEN POCKET HISTORY OF
Irish Writers
FROM SWIFT TO HEANEY

A. Norman Jeffares

THE O'BRIEN PRESS
DUBLIN

First published 1997 by The O'Brien Press Ltd,
20 Victoria Road, Dublin 6, Ireland.
Reprinted twice.
Tel: +353 1 4923333; Fax: +353 1 4922777
E-mail: books@obrien.ie
Website: www.obrien.ie

ISBN: 0-86278-911-7

British Library Cataloguing-in-publication Data
Jeffares, A. Norman (Alexander Norman), 1920-
O'Brien pocket history of Irish writers. - 2nd ed.
1.English literature - Irish authors - History and criticism
2.English literature - 20th century - History and criticism
I.Title
820.9'9415

3 4 5 6 7 8 9 10
05 06 07 08 09 10

Typesetting, editing, layout, design: The O'Brien Press Ltd
Printing: Cox & Wyman Ltd

CONTENTS

INTRODUCTION

The cultural inheritance of Irish men and women writing in English is long and complex. Though this book begins with Jonathan Swift in the 18th century, the historical background of Irish literature reaches back into the aristocratic Gaelic civilisation where poets and monks preserved oral traditions which included genealogies, poems on places, romantic tales in prose, and the sagas of the heroic age (the Ulster and Fenian cycles of tales with all their powerful mythology).

Some of the great manuscript books which survived the Danish raids that disrupted Irish life between 800 and 1014, and the 12th century Anglo-Norman incursion, indicate the wealth of the Gaelic past. Others – such as the beautiful Book of Kells which contains the four gospels exuberantly ornamented and written in an elegant script – indicate the clerical and intellectual resources of Irish medieval Christianity.

Several languages co-existed in Ireland from the 13th century on: Gaelic, the Latin of the Church, Norman-French and English, which was the *lingua franca* of the towns. Many of the early incoming Norman ruling families blended with and adopted the ways of life of the great Irish families with whom they intermarried, notably in their increasing use of Irish and their support of Irish bards. It was, however, a two-way traffic, for the fourth Earl of Kildare, Gerald the Rhymer (d 1398), was probably responsible for the successful introduction of *amour courtois* into the repertory of Irish writers, while there was some translation of Irish material into English (as in *The Book of Howth*, first published in 1871).

The increasing use of Irish by Norman and English

settlers was strongly discouraged by English officialdom. But Irish survived even in the English-speaking regions of 'the Pale', the area controlled by the English-dominated parliament of Dublin. This led, in 1366, to the Parliament passing the Statutes of Kilkenny, designed to prevent English settlers adopting Irish ways of life. These decrees were renewed by Sir Edward Poynings in 1495 and again reinforced by Lord Grey's parliament in 1536.

Confiscation of land and the first plantations of English colonists in Leix and Offaly in 1556 and in Munster in 1586, and of Scots Presbyterians in Ulster in 1603, created fierce divisions, even before Cromwell's final solution of planting all Ireland except Connacht and Clare between 1652 and 1653. The old Gaelic civilisation had virtually collapsed when the last powerful Irish lords left the country in 1607, shortly after Elizabeth I's death, abandoning their struggle against the English, Ireland's liberty having been effectively lost at the Battle of Kinsale in 1601. By now religion had embittered the political situation, for Ireland, unlike England, had not embraced the Protestant Reformation, most of the people remaining loyal to the Catholic Church.

The turmoil of the 17th century wars divided the communities. The Penal Laws, introduced by the Protestant Irish parliament after William of Orange's victories, excluded Catholics from education and the professions. A very large part of the population still used Irish (something remarked on earlier by the traveller Fynes Moryson (1566-1630) and Sir John Davies (1569-1626), sometime Attorney General and Speaker of the Irish parliament, who complained of this 'degenerate' use of the language). However, English was now the language of government, trade and commerce. Irish writers in English were generally of the professional classes and tended to be part of the world of power, the Protestant Ascendancy, and their literary writings did not at first have a specially Irish context. Most of them were brought up within a classical tradition and studied at Trinity College, Dublin, which had been set up by Queen Elizabeth in 1591 as an educational nursery to protect young Irishmen from the Counter-Reformation flourishing in continental universities. Many Irish writers, especially dramatists, sought their audience in the larger market of London. But Irish writing in English turned to Irish subject matters when the Anglo-Irish felt a need to counter unreasonable English treatment of Ireland, the constant appointment of Englishmen to high office in Ireland, the introduction of measures by England which harmed Irish manufacturers and trade (especially in wool and shipping) and which did not help to alleviate but rather increased Irish poverty. This book begins with the first anti-colonial writer, Swift, who, having experienced an influential position at the centre of English political life, resented being treated as a colonial when he returned to Ireland. 'Were not the people of Ireland born as free as those of England?' he asked, and continued: 'Am I a free man in England and do I become a slave in six hours by crossing the Channel?'

Crossing the divide between the two languages and indeed between the two cultures of Ireland began with the antiquarian movement in the latter part of the 18th century, when an interest in Irish music and poetry began to be taken. This accelerated with the success of Thomas Moore's Irish melodies and with the group around George Petrie, who was engaged in the Ordnance Survey of Ireland, which then began to investigate past and current Irish traditions and literature in the 1830s. The great Victorian translators of the 19th century made Irish writing available to those who did not have the language, and the process continues to this day.

In this book translators whose merits are well-established are regarded as part of the history of Irish literature. Some writers in Irish are, perforce, not discussed as they are outside the scope of the book, concentrated as it is upon writing in English. They include authors who represent a vital recrudescence in Irish writing such as Padraic Óg Ó Conaire (1893-1971), Máirtín Ó Cadhain (1906-1970), Seán Ó Riordáin (1916-1977), Eoghan Ó Tuairisc, who also wrote as Eugene Watters (1919-1982), Máire Mhac an tSaoi (b 1922), Eithne Strong (b 1923), Seán Ó Tuama (b 1941). Others of a later generation are considered here. These include Michael Hartnett (b 1941), Micheal Ó Siadhail (b 1947) who writes sensitive verse in both English and Irish, and those known as the *Innti* group (after a journal of that name founded in 1970), including Gabriel Rosenstock (b 1949), Liam Ó Muirthile (b 1950) and, because of the number of excellent translations (including her own) of her work into English, Nuala ní Dhomhnaill (b 1952). Details of these writers' lives and writings can be found in the *Oxford Companion to Irish Literature* (ed Robert Welch, 1996), strongly recommended for its full coverage and blend of factual information and critical judgement.

Inevitably the social (which is almost to say the educational), political and religious backgrounds of Irish writers in English have to be considered, for Irish literature is deeply intertwined with Irish history. The reader is, therefore, referred to an excellent introduction, Breandán Ó hEithir's *A Pocket History of Ireland* (6th edition, revised 1996). Other introductory studies to consider are Máire and Conor Cruise O'Brien, *Ireland, A Concise History* (3rd edition, 1985) and Robert Kee, *Ireland, A History* (1982).

Finally, a word about the purpose of this book. It has been written not only to show the development of Irish writing in English but to convey the enjoyment to be found in it. This depends in part upon its richness and range, its lively achievement, its versatility which is indeed impressive, and in part also, upon the imagination and energy, the skill and integrity of the Irish writers discussed, which imbue their work with unique qualities, reflecting their highly individual attitudes to human life.

A. Norman Jeffares
Fife Ness, 1997

1. THE EIGHTEENTH CENTURY

Rationalism, Anti-Colonialism,
Philosophy and Comedy

JONATHAN SWIFT

The first great Irish writer in English, **Jonathan Swift** (1667-1745), is best known for *Gulliver's Travels* (1726), a savagely satiric view of human society, yet one which has become a children's classic. Lemuel Gulliver, a supposed ship's surgeon, recounts his voyages, the first to Lilliput where he is called the 'Man Mountain' by the diminutive inhabitants. At first he helps them (notably by extinguishing a fire in the Queen's palace by urinating on it) but becomes disillusioned by their way of life, is falsely accused of treason and escapes to Blefuscu, the neighbouring kingdom with which the Lilliputians are at war (this mirrors the longstanding antagonism between England and France).

In Part II Gulliver goes to Brobdingnag where he is minute compared to the gigantic inhabitants; he is disgusted by human anatomy in enlarged form. But his account of English political life, of European politics and warfare disgusts the King of Brobdingnag who considers Gulliver's race 'the most pernicious race of little odious vermin that Nature ever suffered to crawl upon the surface of the Earth'.

After being carried off in his specially built travelling cage by a vast eagle, Gulliver returns to England (which now seems Lilliputian to him!). Then, in Part III, he visits the flying island Laputa and the neighbouring Lagado – a nice anticipation of science fiction. In Laputa the inhabitants are obsessed by speculations about mathematics and music, which Gulliver finds incomprehensible. In Lagado the

Academy of Projectors are engaged in absurd research – one is trying to extract sunbeams out of cucumbers – and Swift obviously enjoys satirising the activities of members of the Royal Society in describing their research activities. The morose Struldbrugs are here too, gloomily resigned to their immortality.

In Part IV Gulliver makes his last voyage, to the land of the Houyhnhnms, horses who run their lives by reason. This is also the land of the degraded Yahoos who are akin to human beings but regarded by the Houyhnhnms as the vilest form of life. After hearing Gulliver's description of European politics they decide he is a Yahoo and he is banished. On his return to England he prefers the company of horses to that of his family.

> As soon as I entered the House, my Wife took me in her Arms, and kissed me; at which, having not been used to the Touch of that odious Animal for so many Years, I fell in a Swoon for almost an Hour. At the Time I am writing, it is five Years since my last Return to *England*: During the first Year I could not endure my Wife or Children in my Presence, the very Smell of them was intolerable; much less could I suffer them to eat in the same Room. To this Hour they dare not presume to touch my Bread, or drink out of the same Cup; neither was I ever able to let one of them take me by the Hand. The first money I laid out was to buy two young Stone-Horses, which I keep in a good Stable, and next to them the Groom is my greatest Favourite; for I feel my Spirits revived by the Smell he contracts in the Stable. My horses understand me tolerably well; I converse with them at least four Hours every day.

Swift's praise of the rational horses and his disgust at the brutal Yahoos have led some commentators to see the last book of the *Travels* as giving an ultimately pessimistic view of human nature, but Swift's own view of humanity is larger than the one his invented character Gulliver puts forward. Gulliver's pride is being satirised. Swift himself combatted the evils of existence with laughter and with exuberant fantastic humour; he balanced his *saeva indignatio*, his fierce anger at the injustice and irrationality of mankind, with compassion and kindness, with his capacity 'for mirth and society'.

In writing to his friend Alexander Pope about *Gulliver's Travels*, he said:

> I have ever hated all nations, professions and communities, and all my love is towards individuals: for instance, I hate the tribe of lawyers, but I love Counsellor Such-a-one, and Judge Such-a-one ... But principally I hate and detest that animal called man, although I heartily love John, Peter, Thomas, and so forth.

Swift had been educated at Kilkenny College and Trinity College, Dublin. He worked as a secretary to Sir William Temple, a retired diplomat living at Moor Park in Surrey, before becoming ordained in the Church of Ireland and taking charge of a parish in Kilroot in Northern Ireland. He did not enjoy being surrounded by dour Presbyterians and returned to work for Temple until the latter's death when he became rector of a parish north of Dublin, this time being surrounded by Roman Catholics. At his advice Esther Johnson, whom he called 'Stella' and had known at Moor Park, moved with her friend Rebecca Dingley to live in Dublin.

Swift visited London in 1701, issuing anonymously there his first political pamphlet, *The Contests and Dissensions between the Nobles and the Commons in Athens and Rome*, in which he praised the Whig leaders. In 1704 *A Tale of a Tub*, which he had begun in Kilroot, attacked abuses in religion. A father leaves his three sons a coat each which

15

they are not to alter in any way. These coats are the Christian faith: the sons are Peter, Martin and Jack, respectively standing for the Catholics, the Anglicans and the Calvinists. Swift thought Roman Christianity too worldly and non-conformism too immoderate; he was himself a churchman of the centre and considered the Anglican church, though imperfect, to be the best because it was the most rational religion he knew.

Swift had now invented his own style, creating a persona whose apparent innocence, varied viewpoint and shattering satiric comments on stupidity have sometimes puzzled his readers.

In *A Tale of a Tub* he lulls his readers into false security, then exposes the falsity of his reasoning. He praises the pursuit of truth, despite the pain this might cause:

> Reason is certainly in the Right; and that in most Corporeal Beings which have fallen under my Cognizance, the *Outside* hath been infinitely preferable to the *In*; Whereof I have been farther convinced from some late Experiments. Last week I saw a Woman *flay'd* and you will hardly believe how much it altered her Person for the worse.

Queen Anne was not amused and Swift's barbs were later to cost him preferment to a bishopric. *The Battle of the Books*, published along with *A Tale of a Tub*, reflects Swift's unease with contemporary corruption of the English language and voices his scepticism about the value of the new sciences. It praises the wisdom of the past, rejecting new intellectual fashions.

From 1707 to 1709 Swift was again in London, seeking in vain as an emissary of the Irish clergy to persuade the Whigs to grant a remission of a tax (the first year's income paid by holders of benefices). When the Tories came to power in 1710 they realised the political power of his blend of cold reason and explosive logic and put him in charge of a journal, *The Examiner*. He became a close friend of the government ministers, Harley and St John, and obtained the concession sought by the Church of Ireland. He did much to get the ministers' policies accepted through his skilful journalism. His anti-war propaganda in *The Conduct of the Allies* largely brought about the end of the war in France and caused the dismissal in 1711 of the conquering Captain-General, the Duke of Marlborough.

In 1713 Swift visited Ireland briefly, to be installed as Dean of St Patrick's Cathedral, a disappointed man because he had failed to obtain a bishopric in Ireland or a deanery in England despite his work for the Tory government. When it fell in 1714 he returned to Dublin determined to keep out of Irish politics but after a few years he took up the cause of Ireland, advocating the greater use of Irish manufacturers. Adopting the persona of a Dublin shopkeeper, M B Drapier, in a series of letters – *The Drapier Letters* – Swift successfully attacked a proposal which would have allowed an English ironmaster, William Wood, to coin copper money ('Wood's halfpence') for Ireland. As a result Swift became a popular hero.

His horror at the widespread poverty of Ireland led to his devastating *A Modest Proposal* (1729) for 'preventing the children of the poor being burdensome and for making them beneficial'. In an apparently matter-of-fact way, he argues a case against poverty as if he were an economist, suggesting that 'a young healthy child, well nursed, is, at a year old, a most nourishing and wholesome food whether stewed, roasted, baked or boiled; and I make no doubt that it will equally serve in a fricasse or ragout.' The scheme is carefully worked out: 'of the 120,000 children computed, 20,000 are to be reserved for breeding', the remaining 100,000 'to be offered for sale at a year old to Persons of Quality and Fortune ... always advising the mothers to let them suck plentifully in the last month so as to render them plump and fat for a good table'. He thought that Irish apathy and greed were as much to blame as English economic policy:

> I grant this food will be somewhat dear, and therefore very *proper for Landlords*; who, as they have already devoured most of the parents, seem to have the best title to the children.

Swift's letters, especially those which make up the *Journal to Stella*, written from London to Esther Johnson, are a delight to read for their directness and vivid, lively wit. In his poetry too, he was concerned to convey truth but that truth had to be presented in concise yet conversational speech. 'A Description of a City Shower' and the 'Humble Petition of Mrs Harris' are good examples. There is plenty of variety among his poems: savage satire on politicians, affectionately teasing poems to Stella, some written for her birthdays, praising her character, her intellect and her kindness, and that strange, long poem *Cadenus and Vanessa* – (Cadenus is an anagram for *decanus*, Latin for dean) which deals with his relationship with Esther Vanhomrigh, whom he called 'Vanessa'.

Against his stern advice, she had followed him from London to Dublin after he became Dean of St Patrick's. She was an attractive girl of twenty, he forty-one, when their intimate friendship began. The poem contrasts her perfections with the imperfections of other women; it tells how Cadenus was surprised at her falling in love with him. He had offered her friendship, he had tutored her, guiding her reading and thinking, but she wants the situation reversed. The poem remains enigmatic. Vanessa, who died in 1723, left instructions in her will for it to be published.

But what success Vanessa met,
Is to the world a Secret yet:
Whether the nymph to please her Swain,
Talks in a high Romantick Strain;
Or whether he at last descends
To like with less Seraphick Ends;
Or, to compound the business, whether
They temper Love and Books together;
Must never to Mankind be told,
Nor shall the conscious Muse unfold.

Other poems record his disgust with untidiness and lack of hygiene; there are playful poems such as the laughing account of his own achievement in 'The Life and Character of Dr Swift' and the supremely comic 'Verses on the Death of Dr Swift', linking himself with the land in which he had not wanted to live. In his will, written in 1745, the year he died, he left money to found a hospital for the mentally ill; and St Patrick's Hospital, the first of its kind, still flourishes. Swift took a keen interest in the planning of it:

He gave the little wealth he had
To build a house for fools and mad:
And showed by one satiric touch
No nation wanted it so much.

GEORGE BERKELEY

Another pupil of Kilkenny College, **George Berkeley** (1685-1753), became a Fellow of Trinity College, Dublin, Dean of Derry and later Bishop of Cloyne. He travelled in Europe, staying in Italy for several years and then, having formed the plan of founding a college in Bermuda and collected promises of funding for it, sailed to Rhode Island in 1729. The plan came to nothing, stultified by Robert Walpole's scepticism and the English Treasury's bureaucratic ineptitude, and Berkeley returned to Ireland in 1731.

A gentle person with a powerful intellect, he wrote his *Principles of Human Knowledge* (1716) with an easy eloquence, disliking the unnecessary obscurity of much learned writing. As a philosopher he opposed John Locke's more mechanical ideas and in his notebooks (labelled *Philosophical Commentaries* by A A Luce, the Berkeleyan scholar) he revealed how he had formed his idea of immaterialism. He believed in the existence of God, the immortality of the soul, and could reconcile God's foreknowledge with the freedom of humanity.

His other work includes his earlier *Essay towards a New Theory of Vision* (1709); *Alciphron, or the Minute Philosopher* (1732), *The Analyst* (1734), *The Querist* (1735) and *Siris* (1744). A major European philosopher by the age of twenty-eight, Berkeley was very conscious of being Irish, to the extent of remarking on several occasions in his *Philosophical Commentaries*, when recording his dissent from various viewpoints (notably of 'the mathematicians'), that 'we Irish men' do not agree. His immaterialism denies that objects exist independently of our perception of them: to exist, he thought, is 'to be perceived'.

Irish Dramatists

WILLIAM CONGREVE

Swift was not the only successful Irish writer in London in the early 18th century. **William Congreve** (1670-1729), his schoolfellow at Kilkenny College and contemporary at Trinity College, Dublin, before he moved to the Inns of Court, made his name with a novel, *Incognita*, a *jeu d'esprit*, which anticipated Fielding's fiction in its detached ironic comedy. It reflected the air and the taste of polite society as did Congreve's most complex play *The Way of* *the World* (1700). He had previously written *The Old Batchelor*, *The Double-Dealer* and the highly successful, riotously funny *Love for Love*. His plays expose illusions; they revolve around money and marriage, the conflicts of youth and age; and they stem from the libertine tradition of comedy which had reacted so strongly against puritanism (the puritan Commonwealth had, after all, closed the theatres in 1642) after the Restoration of Charles II in 1660.

Despite the apparent cynicism of his plays, Congreve included in the famous proposal scene between Millamant and Mirabell what might be seen as a plea for a better kind of marriage than the way of the world would have it.

MILLAMANT: Good Mirabell don't let us be familiar or fond, nor kiss before Folks, like my Lady Fadler and Sir Francis: Nor go to Hide-Park together the first Sunday in a new Chariot, to provoke Eyes and Whispers; And then never to be seen there together again; as if we were proud of one another the first Week, and asham'd of one another ever after. Let us never Visit together, not go to a Play together, but let us be very strange and well bred: Let us be as strange as if we had been marry'd a great while; and as well bred as if we were not marry'd at all.

MIRABELL: Have you any more Conditions to offer? Hitherto your Demands are pretty reasonable.

MILLAMANT: Trifles, – As Liberty to pay and receive Visits to and from whom I please; to write and receive Letters, without Interrogatories or wry Faces on your Part; to wear what I please; and chuse Conversation with regard only to my own Taste; to have no Obligation upon me to converse with Wits that I don't like, because they are your Acquaintance; or to be intimate with Fools, because they may be your Relations. Come to Dinner when I please, dine in my dressing Room when I'm out of Humour without giving a Reason. To have my Closet inviolate; to be sole Empress of my Tea-Table, which you must never presume to approach without first asking leave. And lastly, where-ever I am, you shall always knock at the Door before you come in. These Articles subscribed, if I continue to endure you a little longer, I may by degrees dwindle into a Wife.

More characteristic of restoration wit, however, was the brilliant portrayal of the fifty-five year old widow, Lady Wishfort, as she contemplates how she will receive a possible suitor (actually in the best traditions of comedy, he is Mirabell's servant disguised as 'Sir Roland'):

LADY WISHFORT: Well, and How shall I receive him? In what figure shall I give his Heart the first Impression? There is a great deal in the first Impression. Shall I sit? – No, I won't sit – I'll walk – ay, I'll walk from the Door upon his Entrance; and then turn full upon him – No, that will be too sudden. I'll lye – ay, I'll lye down – I'll receive him in my little Dressing-Room, there's a Couch – Yes, yes, I'll give the first Impression on a Couch – I won't lye neither, but loll and lean upon one Elbow; with one Foot a little dangling off, jogging in a thoughtful way – Yes – and then as soon as he appears, start, ay, start and be surpriz'd, and rise to meet him in a pretty Disorder – Yes – O, nothing is more alluring than a Levee from a Couch in some Confusion – It shews the Foot to advantage, and furnishes with Blushes, and re-composing Airs beyond Comparison. Hark! There's a Coach.

GEORGE FARQUHAR

The taste of the time, however, was changing. **George Farquhar** (1678-1707) developed new ideas, moving the action of his comedies out of the city, away from its smart drawing-rooms and the coffee-houses where the wits congregated, into the country. His most successful plays *The Recruiting Officer* (1706) and *The Beaux Strategem* (1707) are both still popular in our time. There is less straining after smart repartée now, the young men from the city or the army are contrasted with the country characters: bumpkins, constables, the poacher and his mistress, farmers, justices of the peace as well as country gentlefolk. The dashing Captain Plume, for instance, is fundamentally serious:

> No, Faith, I am not that Rake that the World imagines. I have got an Air of Freedom which People mistake for Lewdness in me as they mistake Formality in others for Religion; the World is all a Cheat, only I take mine which is undesign'd to be more excusable than theirs, which is hypocritical; I hurt nobody but my self, but they abuse all Mankind.

Farquhar's plays remain fresh and sparkling, their comic situations are unfolded with confidence, speed and skill.

SIR RICHARD STEELE

Another Irish author, **Sir Richard Steele** (1672-1729), a friend of Swift in London before their quarrelling (mainly for political reasons) in 1712, moved the drama into sentimental comedy with *The Conscious Lovers* (1722). This suited the theatre's new kind of middle-class audiences, for the city-merchant (a character often ridiculed – and cuckolded – in the earlier, more cynical, Restoration comedies written to please an aristocratic audience which took its cue from Charles II's court) has now become a praiseworthy figure, regarded as a suitable match for the children of landowning aristocrats.

Steele is best known, however, for his work in the *Tatler* and *The Spectator*, journals which did much to shape and refine public taste and standards of behaviour in Queen Anne's day, spreading their influence into the countryside where the squire and the parson often relayed their views more widely. Something of Steele's own ebullient character emerges in a letter he sent to Molly Scurlock, whom he sub-sequently married:

> Dear Lovely Mrs Scurlock
>
> I have been in very Good company, where your Health, under the Character of the Woman I lov'd best has been often drank, So that I may say I am Dead Drunk for Your sake, which is more yn I dye for you.
> Svt,
> R. Steele

Other Eighteenth-century Authors

LAURENCE STERNE

Very different to the hearty Steele was **Laurence Sterne** (1713-68), who explored self-knowledge and sentimentality in entirely new ways. Born in Clonmel, he lived as a child in York, Dublin, Derrylossery in Co Wicklow and Car-rickfergus, then spent his life in England, having taken holy orders after being educated at Halifax and Jesus College, Cambridge. He held three livings in Yorkshire, settling into the rectory at Coxwold in 1760. He called it Shandy Hall, having made his name with *The Life and Opinions of Tris-tram Shandy, Gentleman* (1759-67). Sterne is in the line of Rabelais, Cervantes, Sir Thomas Browne and Robert Burton. In this innovative novel he queries most things, upending Locke's ideas of perception and experience by seeming to take them literally, a trick he had learned from Swift's *A Tale of a Tub*:

> I am this month one whole year older than I was this time twelve-month: and having got, as you may perceive, almost into the middle of my fourth volume – and no fur-ther than to my first day's life – 'tis demonstrative that I have 364 days' more life to write just now than when I set

out; so that instead of advancing, as a common writer, in my work with what I have been doing at it – on the contrary, I am just thrown so many volumes back – was every day of my life to be as busy a day as this? – And why not? – and the transactions and opinions of it to take up as much description – And for what reason should they be cut short? As at this rate I should just live 364 times faster than I should write – It must follow, an' please your Worships, that the more I write, the more I shall have to write and consequently, the more your Worships read, the more your Worships will have to read.

Will this be good for your Worships' eyes? It will do well for mine; and, was it not that my opinions will be the death of me, I perceive I shall lead a fine life of it out of this selfsame life of mine; or, in other words, I shall lead a couple of fine lives together.

Sterne was interested in the association of ideas and with the stream of consciousness. He was a model for James Joyce who referred to 'Shandymount' in *Finnegans Wake* and asked 'Did you ever read Laurence Sterne?' He turned literary conventions upside down, treating chronology cavalierly and indulging in digressions, blank pages, black and marbled pages.

Sterne indulges in pedantry only to mock it, serious in his mockery, mocking in his seriousness in this work which contains learning, bawdy and tenderness. There is much humour, joking about Mrs Shandy's complete inability to understand any of her husband's theories. This is no solemn work, then; it can upset the over-serious for Sterne did not want to 'mutilate everything in it down to the prudish humour of every particular'.

He published *The Sermons of Mr Yorick* (1760-1766), Yorick being a character in *Tristram Shandy*, followed by *A Sentimental Journey through France and Italy* (1768) which opens characteristically: 'They order', said I, 'this matter better in France.' The book appeals to the reader to share not only the author's capacity to feel emotion but to enter into the emotions of others. Sterne often breaks off an anecdote; he leaves things in the air, something to be expected, perhaps, of an author who had written in *Tristram Shandy*:

> My good friend, quoth I – as sure as I am I – and you are you
> And who are you? said he. Don't puzzle me: said I.

Sterne's own nature appears in his Journal to Eliza (published as *Yorick to Eliza* (1775)); she was the wife of an East India Company official with whom he had fallen in love and her departure to India caused him great anguish. His ideas tumble out here (rather as Swift's had in his *Journal to Stella*); they are hectic, sentimental, amused and amusing, shrewd and fevered, for Sterne suffered from tuberculosis. A deeply learned man, he may well have learned his basic literary attitudes in his youth in Ireland; certainly he shares self-mockery, narrative skill and the ability to recreate good talk in his writing with such other Irish writers as Swift, Goldsmith and, later, Shaw and Joyce.

OLIVER GOLDSMITH and RICHARD BRINSLEY SHERIDAN

Oliver Goldsmith (1728-1774) was another author who had an extensive influence. He elevated journalism into literature with his essays in *The Bee* and in his urbane series *The Citizen of the World* in which English life is seen through the eyes of a visiting Chinaman, as well as in his hackwork, the histories which remained as successful school texts well into the 19th century. He wrote lyrics with a flowing ease; they include 'When Lovely Woman Stoops to Folly' and the witty 'Elegy on the Death of a Mad Dog':

This dog and man at first were friends;
But when a pique began,
The dog, to gain some private ends,
Went mad, and bit the man.

Around from all the neighbouring streets
The wondering neighbours ran,
And swore the dog had lost his wits,
To bite so good a man.

The wound it seemed both sore and sad
To every Christian eye;
And while they swore the dog was mad,
They swore the man would die.

But sooner a wonder came to light,
That showed the rogues they lied;
The man recovered of the bite,
The dog it was that died.

We remember him for *The Traveller* and *The Deserted Village*, the poignant longer poems that made his name among his contemporaries and are still read and remembered with pleasure. The former combines generalised reflections and personal emotion, the latter encapsulates village life and imbues it with the exile's longing for home:

Dear lovely bowers of innocence and ease,
Seats of my youth, when every sport could please,
How often have I loiter'd o'er thy green,
Where humble happiness endear'd each scene.
How often have I paus'd on every charm,
The shelter'd cot, the cultivated farm,
The never-failing brook, the busy mill,
The decent church that topp'd the neighbouring hill,
The hawthorn bush, with seats beneath the shade,
For talking age and whisp'ring lovers made ...

But above all we remember him for his plays, *The Good Natur'd Man* (1768) and especially *She Stoops to Conquer* (1773), a play based upon his own experience as a school-boy when he lost his way and was misdirected, treating a local squire's house as if it was an inn. The comedy blends absurdity, ironic anticlimax and comic contrivance into a dashing play. With its young man who is shy with ladies but familiar with barmaids, its irascible Squire Hardcastle and his loutish but good-natured stepson Tony Lumpkin, it triumphantly survives the efforts of countless amateur dramatic societies as well as sparkling on the legitimate stage and on the screen.

Drama was a genre that gave many other Irishmen a livelihood in London, where the audiences were. Among them were **Charles Macklin**, author of the lively *Love à la Mode* (1793) with its idiosyncratic Sir Callaghan O'Brallagan, **Arthur Murphy**, known for his farces, **Isaac Bickerstaff**, a successful writer of comic operas, as was **John O'Keefe** with *The Wicklow Gold Mines*. **Hugh Kelly** created many sentimental comedies, his *False Delicacy* (1768) irritating Goldsmith into an essay attacking this form as bastard tragedy.

Goldsmith's own kind of comedy continued to flourish. Two years after *She Stoops to Conquer* came **Richard Brinsley Sheridan's** (1751-1816) *The Rivals*, a play poking fun at fashionable life in Bath. Here are some of the classic ingredients, especially the conflict between youth and age, for Sir Anthony Absolute is a most autocratic father. There are two heroes, young Absolute and his friend Faulkland, and two heroines, Lydia Languish, given to reading sentimental novels from the circulating library, and her foil Julia. Mrs Malaprop confuses language wonderfully and the fiery Irishman Sir Lucius O'Trigger adds to the vitality of the play.

In The School for Scandal (1780) Sheridan stresses the difference between appearances and reality. The main plot is cleverly worked out – mistaken identity; lovers kept apart to be eventually rewarded; the hypocritical natures of Lady Sneerwell and Joseph Surface exposed. The sub-plot of the Teazles, the older husband married to a young wilful wife from the country, is well integrated into the play's action.

Sheridan was a fine theatre manager and became owner of the Drury Lane Theatre in London, only to be ruined when it burnt down in 1809. He had another career as a parliamentarian; he was an impressively eloquent orator, his long speeches in Westminster against Warren Hastings, first Governor-General of British India, impeached in 1787 on charges of extortion, being a *tour de force*.

HENRY GRATTAN and EDMUND BURKE

In his Irish political pamphlets, Swift had been the first powerful anti-colonial writer. He resented the political and especially the economic differences between the two islands, seeing no reason why Ireland should be 'a depending kingdom' at the mercy of Westminster's economic legislation, which, in effect, prevented Ireland exporting to England and crippled its wool trade. 'Burn everything English except their coal,' he proclaimed. His views were echoed later by two outstanding parliamentary orators, **Henry Grattan** (1746-1820), five years older than Sheridan, and **Edmund Burke** (1729-97), twenty-two years younger.

At this time, in the last thirty years of the 18th century, the Protestant Ascendancy, secure in its position of power, had expressed itself in fine public buildings, in plasterwork, in furniture, in glass, in silver, in bookbindings. New theatres were built and painting began to flourish. But

Catholics had no part in the renaissance. Since the beginning of the century, they had been penalised by laws which, while not consistently enforced, denied them the right to own land, to vote, to hold public office, to sit in Parliament, to own a horse worth more than five pounds. A man of liberal vision, Grattan had seen the need for Catholic emancipation, for what in modern times might be regarded as power-sharing. He succeeded in 1782 in getting for Ireland a short-lived independent Parliament. He opened it with the cry 'Spirit of Swift! Spirit of Molyneux', (the William Molyneux whose *The Case of Ireland Stated*, published in 1698, was reputedly burnt by the public hangman), adding that Ireland was now a nation, 'no longer a wretched colony'.

Edmund Burke had gone to study law at the Middle Temple, gravitating there from Trinity College, Dublin, where the Debating Club he founded still flourishes as the College Historical Society. He tried his hand at a literary career, editing the *Annual Register* and writing his influential *A Philosophical Enquiry into the Origin of our Ideas of the Sublime and Beautiful* (1757), before becoming a member of the Westminster parliament at the age of thirty-six. A persuasive orator, a gradualist, essentially a reasonable man, he believed that parliament could ensure the good of a whole society. Indeed, he went further, anticipating modern demands for referenda in a letter advocating parliamentary reform:

> I most heartily wish that the deliberate sense of the kingdom on this great subject should be known. When it is known, it *must* be prevalent. It would be dreadful indeed if there was any power in the nation capable of resisting its unanimous desire, or even the desire of any very great and decided majority of the people. The

people may be deceived in their choice of an object; but I can scarcely conceive any choice they can make to be so very mischievous as the existence of any human force capable of resisting it.

Burke founded his political views on a desire for reform, as his *Speech in Support of Resolutions for Conciliation with the American Colonies* (1775, 1778) shows; he had a deep instinctive distrust of revolution, his eloquent *Reflections on the Revolution in France* (1790) demonstrating this clearly. He had a horror of mob violence exacerbated by the bloodbath that took place in France. He feared that the Westminster parliament by withholding emancipation would drive Irish Catholics into Jacobinism, preventing them from taking part in public life.

His political views on the positions of Catholics have been skilfully analysed by Conor Cruise O'Brien, himself a distinguished critic as well as politician, in *The Great Melody* (1992), a sympathetic biography which includes an annotated anthology of Burke's writings.

The idealism of both Grattan and Burke was, however, overtaken by events. The bloody United Irishmen insurrection of 1798 was followed by the Act of Union of 1800 which abolished the parliament in Dublin and was, in effect, to lead to the end of the power of the Protestant Ascendancy by the close of the 19th century.

THEOBALD WOLFE TONE

Another kind of political eloquence can be found in the attractively forthright journal of **Theobald Wolfe Tone** (1763-1798) one of the revolutionary leaders of the United Irishmen who persuaded the French Directory to attempt an invasion of Ireland. He varies from detachment, when recording the mismanaged French naval expedition to

Ireland of 1796 (which he accompanied), to optimism at a fresh attack and then to a sombre awareness of what was in store for him after his capture in 1798.

2. NINETEENTH-CENTURY FICTION BEFORE THE FAMINE

Nineteenth-century Irish authors were to move a long way from the ironies and satire that were so well expressed in the orderliness, the rationality of 18th century prose. Just as Irish writers of comedy had found their audiences in the London theatre, so Irish writers who expressed themselves in the genre of fiction were often writing mainly for an English audience who knew little about the manners and character of Irish society.

MARIA EDGEWORTH

Maria Edgeworth's (1767-1849) *Castle Rackrent* (1800), is the first regional novel (her Irish novels stimulated Sir Walter Scott's writing about Scotland). Its narrator, the old steward Thady Quirk, tells the story of the decline and fall of five generations of the Rackrent family, feckless, extravagant, generous, autocratic and eccentric. Their estate is finally taken over by Thady's calculating son. The story is told in Hiberno-English, the lively English spoken in Ireland, and appendices, gloss words and comments on Irish customs are provided for the benefit of English readers.

Maria Edgeworth had superb narrative power (no doubt stimulated and sharpened by story-telling to her large family of siblings, stepbrothers and stepsisters) and this propelled her other Irish stories, *Ennui* and *The Absentee*. In *Ormond* (1817) she shows how the hero is pulled by the differing influences of his two uncles, Sir Ulick O'Shane, whose showy hospitality at Castle Hermitage reflects the often excessive hospitality of Irish landlords, and Cornelius O'Shane, an eccentric who seeks enjoyment in a life of social independence, hunting and shooting in the Black Isles, his lawless 'kingdom'.

Maria Edgeworth had set *Castle Rackrent* in the 1780s. But just as her several novels about English life (*Patronage* is the best of them) reflected social life there accurately, her Irish novels show that, through working as her father's assistant on their estate in Longford, she knew her contemporary Ireland and its Hiberno-English speech well. She was a sharp observer of life around her, many of her Irish characters being founded upon people she knew personally.

She was not, however, knowledgeable about Ireland's Gaelic past, in which a new interest was developing in the latter part of the 18th century. This arose out of what might be called an antiquarian interest. **Joseph Cooper Walker** (1761-1810), for instance, represents the widely contemporary curiosity about Celticism; he gave an outline of Irish poetry and music from early times in his *Historical Memoirs of the Bards* (1786), stressing the honour paid to literature in Gaelic society. **Charlotte Brooke** (?1740-1793) (whose father, Henry Brooke (1703-1783), a poet and playwright, is now known for his sentimental novel on education, *The Fool of Quality* (1766-67)) translated heroic poems, odes, elegies and songs in her *Reliques of Irish Poetry* (1789).

LADY MORGAN and CHARLES MATURIN

The Gaelic civilisation, from which both Walker and Brooke drew inspiration, had in effect, lost its vitality, its *raison d'être*, a century and a half earlier after the 'Flight of the Earls' in 1607 when the nobles of the leading Irish clans went into exile. But echoes of it found expression in the

work of two novelists a little younger than Maria Edgeworth. **Sydney Owenson** (?1776-1859), who later became
Lady Morgan, gained contemporary fame with *The Wild
Irish Girl* (1806) in which she adopted the device of having
a young Englishman come to Ireland and meet an Irish girl,
the Lady Glorvina, who instructs him about the past civilisation of Ireland and the present hardships of peasant life. He
is vastly impressed by wild Irish scenery in the west and by
the people he meets, peasants and the Prince of Inishmore
alike. Of course, Glorvina, the Prince's daughter, impresses
him most of all; she knows Irish, sings charmingly and
plays the harp.

The novel blends fashionable Ossianic elements, admiration for the paintings of Salvator Rosa and patriotic
romanticism. Heady stuff, all of it, in those days: success
encouraged Lady Morgan to write other novels, *O'Donnel*
and *The O'Briens and the O'Flahertys*. The latter echoes
Grattan's idealism but blends it with a dash of republican
nationalism in the person of Murrough O'Brien, a patriot
who leaves Ireland after 1798 to become a general in the
French Army.

Hijacking Lady Morgan's success very obviously with a
novel called *The Wild Irish Boy* (1808), **Charles Robert
Maturin** (1782-1824), an eccentric Church of Ireland cler-
gyman, brought in his own interest in Wordsworthianism
and a new attitude to the healing power of nature. In *The
Milesian Chief* (1812) he realises how different life is west
of the Shannon, while his *Women: Pour et Contre* (1818),
the first novel ever to explore an undergraduate's intense
love life, has hints of urban Gothic: these are developed in
Melmoth the Wanderer (1820) into what is one of the most
melodramatic of all Gothic horror novels.

THOMAS MOORE

Lady Morgan and Maturin greatly enjoyed Dublin's social life, the latter finding it advisable to paste a wafer across his lips to prevent himself entering into conversation instead of getting on with his writing. In this liking they were matched by **Thomas Moore** (1779-1859), a friend of Robert Emmet (who advised him not to become involved with the United Irishmen). He left Dublin for the larger stage of London where he became the darling of the drawing rooms. Moore had developed an interest in Irish music at Trinity College, becoming acquainted with the airs that Edward Bunting had collected at a famous gathering of harpers in Belfast in 1792.

Moore knew no Irish but, like Bunting, wanted to preserve Irish music; his way of doing so was to popularise it. He had a fine voice and used to sing the melodic lyrics he wrote which were both fluent and plangent, underpinned by his sure sense of rhyme and rhythm, his range including the sombre as well as the sweet. The sweetness can drift easily into sentimentality but Moore's achievement in the eight volumes of *The Irish Melodies* and the six volumes of his *National Airs* (though sometimes unduly under-rated by modern critics) had a considerable effect upon subsequent Irish writing in English. They can still delight with insouciant variety and control:

> The time I've lost in wooing
> In watching and pursuing
> The light that lies
> In Woman's eyes,
> Has been my heart's undoing.
> Though Wisdom oft has sought me,
> I scorn'd the lore *she* brought me,
> My only books

Were woman's looks,
And folly's all they've taught me.

Moore had first become known in London by translating
Anacreon's lyrics and writing his own amatory poems. His
Lalla Rookh made him a lot of money but is now forgotten,
as his *Memoirs of Captain Rock* should not be. This latter
work, inspired by his reactions to the Ireland of 1818,
attacks British policy in Ireland from the viewpoint of a
Whiteboy (a member of an agrarian secret society given to
intimidation and violence) and is an unusual approach to
the political situation of the time.

Two very different books of reminiscences can be men-
tioned here. **Sir Jonah Barrington**'s (?1760-1834) *Personal Sketches of His Own Times* (2 vols 1827; 3rd vol 1833)
give a rollicking account of a hard-riding, hard-drinking,
duelling gentry, while also conveying the tensions in Ireland before their eruption in 1798. The rebellion of that
year is also treated in the *Leadbeater Papers* by a Quaker,
Mary Leadbeater (1758-1826) whose straightforward
account of life in a Kildare village from 1766 to 1824 is often
moving and always effective.

THE BANIMS, GERALD GRIFFIN and WILLIAM CARLETON

A new generation of novelists explored new kinds of Irish
subject matter. For instance, the **Banim brothers**, **John**
(1798-1842) and **Michael** (1796-1874), wrote twenty-four
books between them, and conveyed a realistic view of Irish
rural life. Admittedly they often dwelt on violent crime in
melodramatic detail but they did know the life of small
farms and country towns intimately. They treated historical
themes with patriotic sentiment. Their *Tales by the O'Hara
Family* (First series, 1825) – the best of them 'Croohore of

the Bill-Hook '– first brought them literary reputation. *The Nowlans* (1826), *The Boyne Water* (1826) and *Father Connell* (1842) are worth reading.

Gerald Griffin (1803-1840) was another author who knew provincial and rural life well. His collection of short stories, *Holland-Tide* (1827), provides plenty of lively examples of the speech of country people. A second collection, *Tales of the Munster Festivals* (1827), enlarges the range of his characters. He is mainly known now for *The Collegians* (1829), a novel based on the actual murder of a girl for which a young man and his boatman were hanged. Against a rich pattern of Irish provincial life the sensational narrative pursues its compelling course, at times melodramatic but convincing in the tragedy it unfolds, of an arrogant yet repentant young man. It was the basis of Dion Boucicault's *The Colleen Bawn* (1860) and Sir Julius Benedict's operetta *The Lily of Killarney* (1862). Like the Banims, Griffin was greatly influenced by Sir Walter Scott: he published more novels and collections of tales but hack work took its toll and he decided to enter a teaching order.

William Carleton (1794-1869) was a much more powerful, more idiosyncratic writer than Griffin or the Banims. Brought up on a farm in Co Tyrone where he heard his mother sing songs in Irish and his father tell traditional tales, he was taught by a hedge schoolmaster. He abandoned his Catholicism and wrote for the Rev Caesar Otway's *Christian Examiner,* notably an account of the Lough Derg pilgrimage in which he adopts a confiding tone though he is led by his self-education into some self-deprecation; it is an account which is still well worth reading. Physically vigorous, Carleton wrote with an energy that matches pre-Famine Ireland with its exuberant vitality, its often violent life overspilling into weddings, dances, faction fights, wakes and funerals. In 'The Battle of the Factions', for instance, he imitates the style of a hedge schoolmaster with its would-be impressive erudition:

'Faith, if an Irishman happened to be born in Scotland, he would find it mighty inconvanient – afther losing two or three grinders in a row – to manage the hard oaten bread that they use there; for which rason, God be good to his sowl that first invented the phaties, anyhow, because a man can masticate them without a tooth at all at all. I'll engage, if larned books were consulted, it would be found out that he was an Irishman. I wonder that neither Pastorini nor Columbkill mentions anything about him in their prophecies consarning the church; for my own part, I'm strongly inclined to believe that it must have been Saint Patrick himself; and I think that his driving all kinds of venomous reptiles out of the kingdom is, according to the Socrastic method of argument, an undeniable proof of it. The subject, to a dead certainty, is not touched upon in the Brehone Code, nor by any of the three Psalters, which is extremely odd, seeing that the earth never produced a root equal to it in the multiplying force of prolification. It is, indeed, the root of prosperity to a fighting people; and many a time my grandfather boasts, to this day, that the first bit of *bread* he ever *ett* was a *phatie*.

Carleton's best work went into *Traits and Stories of the Irish Peasantry* of 1830 and 1833. His first novel, *Fardarougha the Miser* (1839) was followed by several others, of which *Valentine McClutchy* (1845) and *The Black Prophet* (1847) are very telling in their satiric creation of character types. Though the plots are over-contrived and the sensationalism overdone, the comic humour and lively language remind us that he well knew the stresses and strains of rural life when Ireland was in a dangerously divided state, his bilingualism obviously an aid to his understanding. In his verse, too, this emerged in his techniques of assonance and internal rhyming:

> As the white low mist the meadows kissed
> In the summer twilight's glow
> And the otter splashed and the wild duck dashed
> In the sedgy lake below,
> 'Twas sweet to hear the silver bell
> For the flocks on high Dunroe
> From the rail's hoarse throat the ceaseless note
> Would flit, now far, now high,
> And the quavering hum of the snipe would come
> Quick shooting from the sky.

Carleton had a wide following in Ireland – there were over thirty editions, for instance, of his *Willy Reilly and his Dear Colleen Bawn* (1853). He particularly feared the effect of the agrarian secret societies, especially abhorring the Ribbonmen, perhaps because he had been a member of that secret society in his youth. He did much to transmit an oral culture through his writing, his essay on Irish swearing being most useful in its explanations of the oaths and imprecations used so freely by his wide range of characters.

Some authors have wondered why there was not more fiction in 19th century Ireland. Carleton had prophesied, after all, that:

> Banim and Griffin are gone, and I will soon follow them –
> *ultimus Romanorum*, and after that will come a lull, an
> obscurity of perhaps half a century.

The answer is obvious, and William Trevor has put it forcefully in *A Writer's Ireland* (1984):

> All the time in the world was at the disposal of the people
> at the hub of Victoria's empire, bolstered by as much con-
> fidence as the ruling classes could comfortably sustain. It

was the perfect hierarchical environment for long afternoons of cricket, for keeping up the 18th century gardens that were decaying in Ireland, for writing and reading the novels that were edifices in themselves. Ireland, compared, lay in fragments, a battleground for seven centuries, a provincial wilderness beyond the pale of Dublin and the life of the big country houses, sick at heart and with half of its population starving. It had neither the mood nor the stomach for a new art form, just as it hadn't the leisure for the ceremony and subtlety of the game of cricket. Like the novel, that sport has since only intermittently flourished in Ireland.

CHARLES LEVER

Charles Lever (1806-72), influenced by William Hamilton Maxwell's *Wild Sports of the West of Ireland* (1832), produced two early novels that were far removed from Carleton's generally sombre fiction. These were *The Confessions of Harry Lorrequer* (1839) and *Charles O'Malley, the Irish Dragoon* (1841). Lighthearted in their sometimes farcical portrayal of the adventures of young students and subalterns, they convey a delight in abundant hospitality – dining, dancing, drinking; and in sport – shooting, riding, steeplechasing – and in romantic episodes. They were immensely popular, their speed of narrative, their flow of incident and good humour most entertaining.

Lever edited the *Dublin University Magazine* with distinction but nationalists accused him of making his characters into stage Irishmen, always a handy line of attack. Paradoxically, however, Lever's middle and late novels increasingly despair of English people's ignorance of Ireland, their often baffling inability to realise the difference between their own attitudes and traditions and those of Irish people. These novels indicate the Anglo-Irish

Ascendancy's extravagance and apparent decline into self-destruction and their failure to provide political leadership. Lever became more complex and subtle in his treatment of character, his Irish personae more outspoken in their sympathy with the sufferings of the peasantry, their criticisms of English rule in Ireland, and their gloomy view of such matters as land tenure, suburban vulgarity and the way politics were going. *Sir Brooke Fossbrook* (1865) and *Lord Kilgobbin* (1872) are sombre in their analysis of the Ascendancy in decline.

3. ROMANTIC POETRY, NATIONALISM AND THE GOTHIC

While fiction showed an increasing interest in Irish subjects in the 19th century a kindred exploration was also taking place in poetry. Whereas good minor poetry, such as that of **George Darley** and **Aubrey de Vere**, demonstrated some interest in topography, it was largely echoing English romanticism. Less orthodox were **Richard Milliken** and the more sophisticated **Francis Sylvester Mahoney** (who wrote as **Father Prout**) in their burlesqueing of the often absurd style of the hedge schoolmasters, top-heavy with learning. Milliken's 'The Groves of Blarney' and Mahoney's 'The Bells of Shandon' afford, respectively, examples of their ability to capture the insouciant inconsequence of the poems they enjoyed mocking. The inconsequence can be seen in the last stanzas of 'The Groves of Blarney':

> There's statues gracing
> This noble place in –
> All heathen gods
> And nymphs so fair;
>
> Bold Neptune; Plutarch,
> And Nicodemus,

All standing naked
In the open air!

So now to finish
This brave narration
Which my poor genii
Could not entwine;

But were I Homer,
Or Nebuchadnezzar,
'Tis in every feature
I would make it shine.

Straight translations from Irish, however, were beginning to appear. **George Ogle** and **Thomas Furlong** were easily surpassed in rendering Irish originals in English by **Jeremiah Joseph Callanan** (1795-1829). His best poem 'The Outlaw of Loch Lene' captures the emotional vigour of much Irish poetry as well as echoing some of its rhythms, as does his 'Gougane Barra', a poem in praise of a County Cork locale.

JAMES MANGAN and SAMUEL FERGUSON

The Irish poems of **James Clarence Mangan** (1803-49), however, have a novel, highly idiosyncratic intensity. Their flowing lines, their intricate rhyming, their repetitions, their lilting effect make memorable his treatment of Irish subjects in, say, 'The Dark Rosaleen':

I could scale the blue air,
I could plough the high hills,
Oh, I could kneel all night in prayer,
To heal your many ills!
And one ... beamy smile from you
Would float like light between
My toils and me, my own, my true,
My Dark Rosaleen!

My fond Rosaleen!
Would give me life and soul anew,
A second life, a soul anew,
My Dark Rosaleen!

His version of 'O'Hussey's Ode to the Maguire' blends wildness with a singing note:

Though he were even a wolf ranging the round green
    woods,
Though he were even a pleasant salmon in the
    unchainable sea,
Though he were a wild mountain eagle, he could scarce
    bear, he,
This sharp sore sleet, these howling floods.
O, mournful is my soul this night for Hugh Maguire!
Darkly, as in a dream he strays! Before him and behind
Triumphs the tyrannous anger of the wounding wind,
The wounding wind, that burns as fire!
It is my bitter grief – it cuts me to the heart
That in the country of Clan Darry this should be his fate!
O, woe is me, where is he? Wandering, houseless,
    desolate,
Alone, without or guide or chart!

Other of his Irish poems are 'The Woman of the Three Cows', 'Kinkora' and the 'Lament for the Princes of Tir Owen and Tirconnell'. He also wrote idiosyncratic and highly impressive poems such as 'Gone in the Wind', 'The Nameless One', 'Twenty Golden Years Ago', 'Siberia' and 'The Time of the Barmecides'.

Mangan's interest in Irish subjects stemmed from his working in the Ordnance Survey for ten years. Whether he translated from Irish originals or used others' prose versions is not clear, but he was able to invest them with both passion and plangency. An eccentric addicted to alcohol and later to opium, introspective, lonely and despairing, he died at a relatively young age in a cholera epidemic.

Very unlike Mangan's romanticism was the achievement of **Sir Samuel Ferguson** (1810-86) who was not entirely the establishment figure he is sometimes made out to be. Married to a member of the Guinness family, Deputy Keeper of the Records, knighted and a President of the Royal Irish Academy, Ferguson wanted reconciliation between nationalists and unionists, between Catholics and Protestants in Ireland and sought it by making ancient Irish culture available, however suspect this might make him in Ascendancy society.

He began, like Mangan, by writing for the journals, notably the *Dublin University Magazine*. His translations – 'Uileacan Dubh Ó', 'The Lapfull of Nuts', 'Cashel of Munster' and 'The Fairy Thorn', for example – arose out of his deep knowledge of Irish culture and literary achievement in the heroic, pagan period. His sense of humour got its head in 'Father Tom and the Pope', later balanced by 'The Loyal Orangeman' and 'At the Polo Ground'. His *Lays of the Western Gael and Other Poems* (1865) contained pieces from the journals as well as new work based on material from the legends. 'Congal' is typical of his epic poetry which lacks a sensuous quality though it possesses accuracy and a measured, masculine force. 'Deirdre's Lament for the Sons of Usnach' is probably his best treatment of heroic legend. It opens starkly and develops into effective repetition quickly:

> The lions of the hill are gone,
> And I am left alone – alone –
> Dig the grave both wide and deep,
> For I am sick, and fain would sleep.
>
> The falcons of the wood are flown,
> And I am left alone – alone –

> Dig the grave both deep and wide,
> And let us slumber side by side.

Deirdre celebrates Naoise with whom she ran away, then cries for vengeance upon King Conor (who had Naoise and his brothers treacherously murdered when they were under safe conduct) before concluding in the opening tone of the poem:

> Dig the grave both wide and deep,
> Sick am I and fain would sleep!
> Dig the grave and make it ready,
> Lay me on my true love's body.

Some of Ferguson's Celtic heroes ran the risk of seeming Victorian gentlemen but 'The Welshmen of Tirawley' (in which the captive Welshmen, offered the alternatives of being blinded or castrated, chose blindness) reveals him as able at times to match the factual ruthlessness of his originals. He could be simple very effectively indeed in such poems as 'The Fair Hills of Ireland' and 'Ceann Dubh Deelish' while 'The Fairy Thorn', a rendering of an Ulster ballad, marked a new achievement in repetitive rhetoric, an eerie poem that shows his capacity for imaginative interpretation. He had a Keatsian ability to combine words into new, effective compound adjectives – 'seedclasping', 'wrathful soaring' – which enriched his powerful, moving 'Lament for the Death of Thomas Davis':

> I walked through Ballinderry in the spring-time,
> When the bud was on the tree;
> And I said, in every fresh-ploughed field beholding
> The sowers striding free,
> Scattering broadside forth the corn in golden plenty
> On the quick seed-clasping soil
> Even such, this day, among the fresh-stirred hearts of Erin,
> Thomas Davis, is thy toil!'

THOMAS DAVIS and JOHN MITCHEL

Thomas Davis (1814-45), whose early death Ferguson lamented, was one of the founders of *The Nation*, an influential weekly which reached a readership estimated at a quarter of a million. It put to its audience the nationalist views of the Young Ireland party as well as encouraging an interest in the Irish past. Davis himself wrote rhetorical propagandist ballads for it such as 'A Nation Once Again'.

More extreme in his views, **John Mitchel** (1815-75), who edited the journal in 1847 (it was suppressed in 1848, to re-emerge in a second, more moderate series in 1849), wrote in a satirical style reminiscent of Thomas Carlyle. He founded the revolutionary journal *United Irishman* in 1848 (to which Mangan contributed); and, after he was convicted of treason-felony and deported to Bermuda, South Africa and Tasmania, and had finally escaped, wrote his classic, forceful and forthright *Jail Journal, or Five Years in British Prisons* (1854).

The Famine

In the year Davis died, 1845, the Great Famine began: the potato crop was afflicted by a fungus that year and again in 1846 and 1848 (the acreage was reduced in 1847). It is estimated that about one-and-a-half million people died as a result of this failure of the crop that supplied half the population with its food and that another one-and-a-half million emigrated between 1845 and 1851.

The Famine was a watershed. The lively exuberant life of the previously populous countryside described by the early novelists changed: emigration left large areas deserted and desolate. Early marriage could no longer be supported on small holdings of land devoted to the growth of potatoes, and land tenure became a more vital issue than before – as Carleton demonstrated in three of his novels *Valentine M'Clutchy, the Irish Agent* (1845), *The Black Prophet* (1847) and *The Emigrants of Ahadarra* (1848).

While fighting for Catholic emancipation (which was achieved in 1829) Daniel O'Connell (1775-1847) had urged the learning of English for political and economic reasons; and the system of National Schools, set up in 1830, compelled the use of English as a medium of instruction. Political pressure led to the Tenant League, founded in 1850, which fought for the famous Three Fs; fair rent, free sale and fixity of tenure. In this Land War members of the secret Fenian movement, founded in 1858, joined the Land League, founded in 1879, emphasising a need for it to become more militant. These various factors, economic, educational and political, as well as the Jansenist puritanism ushered in by Father Theobald Mathew, the advocate of temperance, did not provide a milieu which encouraged much in the way of literature. Indeed the two decades after the Famine do not reveal much new talent.

SHERIDAN LE FANU and BRAM STOKER

There were, however, some notable exceptions. **Sheridan Le Fanu** (1814-1873), the editor and owner of several Dublin journals, whose mysteries and ghost stories made him a bestseller, continued the Gothic strain. He displayed a complex psychological investigation of characters under stress in such novels as *The House by the Churchyard* (1863) and *Uncle Silas* (1884) which carried horror to new heights, perhaps only surpassed a dozen years later by **Bram Stoker's** *Dracula*. Stoker (1847-1912), who proved an excellent theatre manager for Sir Henry Irving, wrote other novels, the best of these being the sinister *The Lair of the White Worm*, though none of them matched the spine-chilling ghoulish excitement of Count Dracula's misdeeds, based on European vampire legends but firmly located in the 19th century.

CHARLES KICKHAM, WILLIAM ALLINGHAM and SAMUEL LOVER

Charles Joseph Kickham (1828-1882) was greatly affected by what he read in *The Nation*. He joined the Tenant League and later the Fenians. His ten novels were committed to the nationalist cause, notably *Sally Cavanagh* (1869), an exploration of peasant suffering, and *Knockna-gow* (1873), his best-known work, an attack on the corruption inherent in the system of land tenure.

William Allingham's (1824-89) long poem *Lawrence Bloomfield in Ireland* (1864) reads almost like fiction in its approach to the tensions of Irish life, for Allingham, a reformist, drew a picture of a liberal young landlord in his character Bloomfield as well as portraying the secret society of Ribbonmen and good and bad land agents. Allingham, of course, is better known for his shorter poems about Ballyshannon (such as 'The Winding Banks of Erne') in which he lists place names with evident pleasure: 'From Portnasun to Balliebawns, and round the Abbey Bay/From rocky Inis Saimer to Cool-nargit sandhills grey ...') where he grew up and for a time worked in the Customs Service, as well as for the often anthologised poem about the fairies, 'Up the Airy Mountain':

> Up the airy mountain
> Down the rushy glen
> We daren't go a-hunting
> For fear of little men;
> Wee folk, good folk
> Trooping all together;

Green jacket, red cap
And white owl's feather.

While the stage Irishman appeared as a butt in such novels of **Samuel Lover** (1797-1868) as *Handy Andy* (1842), there was a change for the better in the treatment of this stock character in the lively and extremely successful melodramas written and staged by **Dion Boucicault** (1820-1890), among them *The Colleen Bawn* (1860), modelled on Griffin's novel *The Collegians, Arrah-na-Pogue* (1864) and *The Shaughraun* (1875). Boucicault, a prolific playwright and innovative actor-manager, who experienced a spectacular, switchback series of financial successes and reverses, exerted a powerful effect on 19th century theatre. He was much admired by Shaw and later by O'Casey; though his boastful stage-Irish heroes still drink they are less caricatures than before and can be both efficient and (deliberately) amusing.

4. SOCIAL COMEDY WITH A MESSAGE
Wilde and Shaw: Wits Abroad

New talents were to emerge in the 1880s: **Oscar Wilde** (1854-1900), **George Bernard Shaw** (1856-1950), **George Moore** (1852-1933) and **William Butler Yeats** (1865-1939). Wilde and Shaw were to achieve their greatest successes in writing plays in the tradition of social comedy. Like so many of their Irish predecessors these Dubliners sought their audiences in London and gave them a picture of English life. Both of the men used wit and paradox and they often inverted orthodox traditions.

They had, however, messages to put across, and they increased the impact of their writing with a strong awareness of the value of publicity. Wilde preached the doctrine of aestheticism, Shaw that of Fabian socialism. Wilde described George Moore as conducting his education in public, and Moore certainly shared Wilde's and Shaw's capacity for self-promotion and irreverence, his awareness of social injustice giving strength to his early, realistic fiction.

W B Yeats, too, realised the need for publicity in order to project his views. The general climate of ideas in the 1890s affected all these writers, just as they themselves did much in their different ways to shape public attitudes. Of the four Yeats was most concerned to change attitudes in Ireland, and his role in the history of Ireland's literature is correspondingly more significant and will receive slightly longer treatment here.

OSCAR WILDE

These four writers had to serve their apprenticeships. Wilde wrote poems, stories and criticism, notably 'The Decay of Lying' and 'The Critic as Artist'; his essays and dialogues were collected in *Intentions* (1891). His novel *The Picture of Dorian Gray* first appeared in 1890; it showed his superb sense of style and was sophisticatedly decadent, exuding a sense of evil. His reputation as conversationalist, wit and dandy, as aesthete and public lecturer, was based upon an excellent education and supported by successful journalism.

His plays of the early nineties, *Lady Windermere's Fan* (1892), *A Woman of No Importance* (1893), *An Ideal Husband* (1895) and *The Importance of Being Earnest* (1895) were in the long line of social comedy that stretches from the theatres of Greece and Rome through those of the Restoration and on into Victorian England. Wilde brought a lighthearted cynicism and sophisticated irony into his view of the conventions of the English upper classes, inverting them, as in the opening of *The Importance of Being Earnest*:

ALGERNON: [...] Oh! [...] by the way, Lane, I see from your book that on Thursday night, when Lord Shoreman and Mr Worthing were dining with me, eight bottles of Champagne are entered as having been consumed.

LANE: Yes, sir; eight bottles and a pint.

ALGERNON: Why is it that at a bachelor's establishment the servants invariably drink the Champagne? I ask merely for information.

LANE: I attribute it to the superior quality of the wine, Sir. I have often observed that in married households the Champagne is rarely of a first-rate brand.

ALGERNON: Good heavens! Is marriage so demoralising as that?

He brought the use of paradox to new levels in the witty conversations of his characters:

ALGERNON: I hope to-morrow will be a fine day, Lane.

LANE: It never is, Sir.

ALGERNON: Lane, you're a perfect pessimist.

LANE: I do my best to give satisfaction, Sir.
[...]

JACK: If you don't take care, your friend Bunbury will get you into a serious scrape one day.

ALGERNON: I love scrapes. They are the only things that are never serious.

JACK: Oh, that's nonsense, Algy. You never talk anything but nonsense.

ALGERNON: Nobody ever does.

Wilde was imprisoned for two years for homosexual offences:

To drift with every passion till my soul
Is a stringed lute on which all winds can play,
Is it for this that I have given away
Mine ancient wisdom, and austere control?
Methinks my life is a twice-written scroll
Scrawled over on some boyish holiday
With idle songs for pipe and virelay,
Which do but mar the secret of the whole.
Surely there was a time I might have trod
The sunlit heights, and from life's dissonance
Struck one clear chord to reach the ears of God:
Is that time dead? Lo! with a little rod
I did but touch the honey of romance –
And must I lose a soul's inheritance?

Out of his experience of hard labour in Pentonville, Wandsworth and Reading gaols came *The Ballad of Reading Gaol* (1898), a most moving poem which uses repetition in a devastating way in its account of a hanging. He knows why the condemned man looked upon the garish day:

With such a wistful eye;
The man had killed the thing he loved,
And so he had to die

The poem's final stanza, in the sixth section, returns to the idea:

And all men kill the thing they love,
By all let this be heard,
Some do it with a bitter look,
Some with a flattering word,
The coward does it with a kiss,
The brave man with a sword

De Profundis (1905; the suppressed part was published in 1949, the original version appearing in 1962), a bitter attack on Lord Alfred Douglas and his father the Marquess of

Queensberry in which he discusses the treatment of prisoners and ex-prisoners and meditates on his own self-deception, offers an apologia for his life and its relationship to the art and culture of his time.

GEORGE BERNARD SHAW

Shaw took some time to find himself as a playwright. At first he tried unsuccessfully to shine as a novelist, four of his five novels (the best is *Cashel Byron's Profession*) being serialised in periodicals between 1884 and 1888. Like his plays, they analysed politics and the English class system as well as looking amusedly at the foibles of English society. His music, art and theatre criticism, however, established him in London's literary world, *The Quintessence of Ibsenism* (1891) and *The Perfect Wagnerite* (1895) both being impressive books. Shaw became converted to socialism and joined the Fabian Society, teaching himself to become an effective public speaker, writing many pamphlets in support of his principles, which included women's rights and a reform of the voting system.

Widowers' Houses (1893), the first of the four plays of *Plays Pleasant and Unpleasant* (1896), like *Mrs Warren's Profession* (written in 1893), attacked the social evils beneath the respectability of Victorian bourgeois prosperity and the stifling codes of gentility and good taste. It portrayed the reality of tenements, brothels, prostitution, bad working conditions in factories – the exploitation of the working class, in short, which was the target for his thoughtful reforming drama. Understandably, it surprised many members of his audiences, utterly unused to hearing two sides of a social problem argued on stage. *Arms and the Man* (1894) was typical of his technique in its comic reversal of conventional concepts of love and war. His ability to surprise, to take a satirical view of stereotyped ideas and beliefs made his *John Bull's Other Island* (first performed in 1904; published in 1907) very successful commercially.

The heroine of the play has been waiting for Larry Doyle, a somewhat bitter Irish realist, to propose to her, but she finally falls for a sentimental Englishman, Broadbent, whose progressive plans for Roscullen are characterised finally as a 'foolish dream of efficiency'. Doyle sees dreaming as the root of Ireland's troubles:

> But your wits can't thicken in that soft moist air, on those white springy roads, in those misty rushes and brown bogs, on those hillsides of granite rocks and magenta heather. You've no such colours in the sky, no such lure in the distances, no such sadness in the evenings. Oh, the dreaming! the dreaming! the torturing, heart-scalding, never satisfying dreaming, dreaming, dreaming, dreaming!

Shaw said that when he took a subject about which his contemporaries sang sad songs he pursued it to a logical conclusion and it inevitably 'resolved itself into comedy'.

He wrote a series of challenging prefaces to his plays as well as explicit stage directions which emphasised the plays' generally anti-romantic themes. Their range developed impressively. In *Candida*, for instance, came Shaw's first emphasis on an unusual independent-minded heroine, followed up by those of *Major Barbara* (1907) and then *Saint Joan* (1924), in the opinion of many his best play. In it Warwick sums up the intellectual and spiritual problems that Shaw found in the story of Saint Joan; he describes her position as:

> the protest of the individual soul against the interference of priest or peer between the private man and his God. I should call it Protestantism if I had to find a name for it.

Shaw was skilled in bringing historical subjects to life as in *The Devil's Disciple* and *Caesar and Cleopatra*. In the Preface to the latter he said his remarks could bear no other construction than 'an offer of my Caesar to the public as an improvement on Shakespeare's. And, in fact, that is their precise purport.'

His *Man and Superman* (1905) expressed his ideas about the Life Force, based upon a belief in Creative Evolution, a theory that individuals, through intelligence, imagination and will-power, would, he hoped, improve the quality of human life. On the other hand, his dialectical balance emerged in some sceptical, ironic pessimism about human nature, influenced by the First World War with which *Heartbreak House* (1922) deals so well. His use of discussion increased in the cycle of *Back to Methuselah* (1921). So, too, as did his audiences, for he had not only won acceptance for himself as a witty and provocative pundit but for his particular kind of drama, which despite its wit and humour, its unorthodoxy and powerful use of paradox, was profoundly serious. He makes his audiences aware of the complex, unpredictable nature of humanity and he does this with convincing confidence. A prolific author of more than fifty plays, Shaw's prose, always clear and effective, subtly allusive, contains *The Intelligent Woman's Guide to Socialism and Capitalism* (1928) and *Everybody's Political What's What* (1944). His correspondence was extensive and entertaining.

5. SERIOUSNESS AND HUMOUR IN THE NOVEL

GEORGE MOORE

Experiment and innovation were in the air. **George Moore** (1852-1933), who had intended to become an artist and studied in the Paris of Degas and Manet, of Dujardin and Zola, turned to literature instead. His *Confessions of a Young Man* (1888) convey something of his self-consciously unorthodox life in Paris. He gradually developed his skill as a novelist. *A Modern Lover* (1883) and the Zola-esque *A Mummer's Life* (1884) were followed by the Balzacian *Esther Waters* (1894), his first major achievement, which brought naturalism into English fiction as well as Moore's knowledge of horse-racing and betting (his father, a Mayo landlord, the owner of a large estate, had kept a racing stable). The human drama of the novel was, he said, the story of a servant girl with an illegitimate child saved from the baby farmers and, despite endless temptation, successfully brought up. Other novels followed, including *Evelyn Innes* (1898) and *Sister Teresa* (1901). When he returned to Ireland in 1900, to find new subject matter and a new way of writing, it was with an already distinguished literary reputation.

Moore had, of course, already written on Irish subjects, *Parnell and His Island* (1887) alienating nationalist opinion, for Moore, having succeeded his father as a landlord, was contemptuous of the peasantry. *A Drama in Muslin* (1886), however, had irritated landowners with its picture of the insecurity of their position during the period of the Land League and its portrayal of the plight of the 'muslin marytrs', the daughters of the Ascendancy for whom marriage was the only career.

Moore disapproved of the Boer War and, with the prospect of change attractive at this stage of his career, left England to join in the Irish literary movement. He helped in the production of its first two plays. He reworked a play by his cousin Edward Martyn, *The Tale of the Town*, quarrelled with Yeats over their joint venture, *Diarmuid and Grainne* and wrote the stories of *The Untilled Field* (1903) in imitation of Turgenev, contrasting dream and reality in bleak accounts of life in the poverty-stricken areas of Mayo. He followed these stories with *The Lake* (1903), a novel in which he created his own style, what he called the melodic line, through which he develops a self-questioning drama in the mind of a priest whose morals are attuned to nature:

> He walked along the shore feeling like an instrument that had been tuned. His perception seemed to have been indefinitely increased, and it seemed to him as if he were in communion with the stones in the earth and the clouds in heaven; it seemed to him as if the past and the future had become one.
>
> The moment was one of extraordinary sweetness, never might such a moment happen in his life again. The earth and sky were enfolding in one tender harmony of rose and blue, the blue shading down to grey, and the lake floated amid vague shores, vaguely as a dream floats through sleep. The swallows were flying high, quivering overhead in the blue air. There was a sense of security and persuasion and loveliness in the evening.

Moore delighted in shocking people. In 1904 he quarrelled for the third time with Mrs Craigie, an American heiress, with whom he seems to have fallen in love, and who dismissed him. Moore had his revenge, as he told his friend Edouard Dujardin. His biographer Joseph Hone tells the story.

'I was walking in the Green Park', he said, 'and I saw her in front of me. I was blind with rage and I ran up behind her and kicked her.' At first he related this story with some embarrassment, but when he grew accustomed to his invention, with relish. The scene in the Green Park was afterwards used in the sketch, *'Lui et Elle'* ... where a heartless woman on whose face he detected a mocking smile, receives the assault 'nearly in the centre of the backside, a little to the right', and seems highly gratified to find that she has aroused such a display of feeling. 'It was inevitable, I said, part of the world's history, and I lost sight of all things but the track of my boot on the black crêpe de Chine.'

Moore's masterpiece was to come at the end of his stay in Dublin. In the three volumes of *Hail and Farewell* (1911-14) he gave his ironic portrayals of the literary movement and of those who brought it about. He mocked, he gossiped, he was malicious; but he was also critically perceptive. Anecdote, vignette and reverie were woven into a witty tapestry. Here is an example, a malicious account of how the distinguished Dublin surgeon, Sir Thornley Stoker, collected his antiques:

> ... on the trail of a Sheraton sideboard and Naylor has been asked to keep it till an appendix should turn up. The Chinese Chippendale mirror over the drawing-room chimney-piece originated in an unsuccessful operation for cancer; the Aubusson carpet in the back drawing-room represents a hernia; the Renaissance bronze on the landing a set of gall-stones; the King Cloisonnee a floating kidney; the Buhl cabinet his opinion on an enlarged liver; and Lady Stoker's jewels a series of small operations performed over a term of years.

Moore was anticipating the modern genre of 'faction', for his literary art shaped fact with the skills of the writer of fiction. He was disillusioned with Irish Catholicism, with the blend of that Catholicism with Gaelic nationalism and he did not hide his views. It was time to leave but his stay in Dublin had not harmed his own art.

After he established himself at Ebury Street in London he wrote two particularly fine books, *The Brook Kerith* (1916) and *Heloise and Abelard* (1921). The first is Moore's fascinating retelling of the New Testament; in this Jesus lives on after the crucifixion as a shepherd among the Essenes where Paul discovers him and holds surprising conversations with him:

> And seating himself on a smooth stone Paul watched Jesus's hand tying new thongs, wondering if the madman's mind was still set on Jerusalem and if he would go thither as soon as he [Paul] was safely out of the ways of the Jews. Each shut himself within the circle of his own mind, and the silence was not broken till Paul began to fear that Jesus was plotting against him; and to distract Jesus's mind from his plots, if he were weaving any, he began to compare the country they were passing through with Galilee, and forthright Jesus began to talk to Paul of Peter and John and James, sons of Zebedee, mentioning their appearances, voices, manner of speech, telling of their boats, their fishing tackle, the fish-salting factory of Magdala, Dan, and Joseph his son. He spoke a winning story of the fishing life round the lake, without mention of miracles, for it was not to his purpose to convince Paul of any spiritual power he might have.

The second tells the story of the ill-fated lovers, set against a complex background. There were other autobiographical writings, *Avowals* (1919), *Conversations in Ebury Street* (1924) and the posthumous *A Communication to my Friends* as well as other volumes of fiction. Moore had experimented and revised incessantly; he enjoyed the art of narration and he conveyed that enjoyment very effectively indeed.

EMILY LAWLESS

Emily Lawless (1845-1913) had also, like Moore, written about agrarian crime in the Land War period in her novel *Hurrish* (1886). In *Grania* (1892) she recounted the plight of a girl in what she viewed as the predominantly masculine world of an Aran island, and her *With Essex in Ireland* (1896) attempted to portray the Elizabethan campaign of 1575 through an Englishman's diary. She wrote some five poems, included in *With the Wild Geese* (1902), which demonstrate her rapport with the wild places of the west, the struggle to earn a living there or to emigrate:

> See, beneath us our boat
> Tugs at its tightening chain,
> Holds out its sail to the breeze,
> Pants to be gone again.
> Off then with shouts and mirth,
> Off with laughter and jests,
> Mirth and song on our lips
> Hearts like lead in our breasts.

SOMERVILLE and ROSS

An outstanding achievement in fiction based on Irish life was the work of two women writers, the cousins **Edith Oenone Somerville** (1858-1949) and **Martin Ross** (the pseudonym of **Violet Martin** (1862-1915). The former, trained as an artist, was a member of a family long established at Castletownshend in southwest Cork, the latter of one settled in Oughterard, Co Galway.

Their first novel was *An Irish Cousin* (1889), intended as a Gothic horror story; of the four novels that followed, *The*

Real Charlotte (1894) is a masterpiece in which the decay of the Ascendancy is seen against other aspects of Irish life. The action largely stems from the ambitious plans of Charlotte Mullen, scheming, ruthless, greedy and acquisitive in her social climbing and other ambitions. Her evil nature affects the other characters: Francie, her vulgar, high-spirited niece, loved by the weak Christopher Dysart of the Big House but thrust into the arms of Hawkins, an insensitive soldier; and the married land agent Lambert, who loves her. Charlotte herself has passionate designs upon Lambert (the death of whose wife she causes) but these come to nothing after Francie's death. This is a powerful, tragic story, shot through with deft comic touches. Superb descriptions of the countryside, precisely observed, set the emotive scenes brilliantly. Human behaviour is equally sharply observed and its crucial flows remorselessly explored.

In their vastly successful Irish RM series – *Some Experiences of an Irish RM (1899); Further Experiences of an Irish RM* (1908) and *In Mr Knox's Country* (1915) – Somerville and Ross place an Englishman, Major Yeates, in a West Cork village and recount the hilarious escapades in which he finds himself, especially through the machinations of Flurry Knox. The wide range of characters, notably old Mrs Knox, Mrs Cadogan and Slipper, are drawn with precision, their eccentricity prized. 'The House of Fahy', one of their best stories, features Maria, a dog whose activities make her a constant menace. Mrs Cadogan, the cook, sets the tone of the story with an account of a crime that is minor compared to what is to follow:

> 'I can't put a thing out o' me hand but he's watching me to whip it away!' declaimed Mrs Cadogan, with all the

disregard of her kind for the accident of sex in the brute creation. ''Twas only last night I was back in the scullery when I heard Bridget let a screech, and there was me brave dog up on the table eating the roast beef that was after coming out from the dinner!'

'Brute!' interjected Philippa, with what I well knew to be a simulated wrath.

'And I had planned that bit of beef for the luncheon,' continued Mrs Cadogan in impassioned lamentation, 'the way we wouldn't have to inthrude on the cold turkey! Sure he has it that dhragged, that all we can do with it now is run it through the mincing machine for the Major's sandwiches.'

The idiosyncratic speech is original and the witty dialogue arises naturally from the comic situations which gain their force from the detached almost dead-pan style of narration. This is the comedy of manners given a new ambiance, a world where social gradations are minute and highly complex but where horses, their performances – and their prices – can have a levelling effect. The stories, however, are not only superbly funny but reflect the awareness of country people of the serious side of life.

This aspect was stressed after Martin Ross's death in *The Big House at Inver* (1925), a story earlier suggested by her in a letter to her cousin describing the decline of a family: its sombre account of a powerful character dominated by hatred has its touches of comedy. Comedy is, almost of necessity, captured in the writings of Somerville and Ross, but they continue to capture it with compassion, for their detachment was balanced by a delight in vigorous life, catastrophes and all.

PERCY FRENCH

Something of the spirit of Somerville and Ross irradiates the writings of **Percy French** (1854-1920), born in Roscommon and educated at Trinity College, Dublin. He first earned his livelihood as a civil engineer, having become known for his music hall song 'Abdallah Bubbul Ameer', written when he was a student, followed by his ever-popular ballad 'The Mountains of Mourne'. French's humorous stories, which use Hiberno-English to great effect, gave him an international reputation. These appeared in *The First Lord Liftinant and Other Tales* (1890). His songs have an attractive and lasting lightness of touch; they include 'Phil the Fluter's Ball', 'Come Back, Paddy Reilly' and the song about the West Clare Railway (which led to a libel action with the directors of the company), 'Are ye Right There, Michael?':

> Are ye right there, Michael? Are ye right?
> Do ye think that we'll be there before the night?
> Ye've been so long in startin
> That ye couldn't say for sartin –
> Still ye might now, Michael, so ye might ...
>
> Kilkee! Oh, you'll never get near it!
> You're in luck if the train brings you back,
> For the permanent way is so queer,
> It spends most of its time off the track.

GEORGE BIRMINGHAM

Equally active and equally valuing the comic spirit was **George A Birmingham** (1865-1950), the pseudonym of Rev J O Hannay, who wrote learned books such as *The Spirit of Christian Monasticism* (1903) and *The Wisdom of the Desert* (1904) under his own name. He led a varied life: from being Rector of Westport, Co Mayo, where the action of several of his novels takes place, he served abroad in several countries as an embassy chaplain until 1924 when he went to a parish in Somerset, moving thence to one in London in 1934. He began writing comic novels in 1905, achieving a popular success with *Spanish Gold* (1908). The main character, the Rev J J Meldon, offhand-edly wise and witty, was founded upon a real-life eccentric character. He wrote in all nearly sixty novels.

An enthusiastic member of the Gaelic League, from which he was later ejected, Birmingham wrote several political novels analysing Irish politics, the best of them *The Red Hand of Ulster* (1912), a sombre assessment of the political situation in Northern Ireland. He sought compromise and tolerance, but his *General John Regan* (1913) which contains a Meldon-like character in the shrewd local doctor, O'Grady, caused a riot in Westport when it was staged there in 1914.

A man of large outlook, particularly tolerant and profoundly serious in his politics, Birmingham was surprised by the nationalists' over-sensitive reaction to his ironic and satiric treatment of country people, particularly cunning peasants. The parallel with public reactions to Synge's plays a few years earlier – and to O'Casey's in the twenties – is clear.

Accusations of bigotry must have been painful; to read his novels now is to recognise and enjoy a civilised humour, which is in the vein of Sterne's *Tristram Shandy*. His books explore the results of misunderstandings and display ingenuity and wit in the way such situations are sorted out by the wiser, more realistic characters. Birmingham was still writing entertainingly in his early eighties.

JEREMIAH O'DONOVAN and OTHER NOVELISTS

George Moore's naming the priest Oliver Gogarty in his novel *The Lake* had caused the real, young Oliver St John Gogarty, who was to become a leading Dublin medical specialist and author, some embarrassment; what if his pious and stern mother was to read the novel? But the model was not so much Gogarty but **Jeremiah O'Donovan** (1871-1942) who wrote six unduly neglected novels as Gerald O'Donovan. A progressive priest, O'Donovan supported the Gaelic League and the Irish Agricultural Organisation and was instrumental in getting artists to work on a new cathedral in Loughrea of which he was administrator. He worked there until 1904 when the conservatism of a new bishop led him to leave the priesthood.

Father Ralph (1913) is the best of his novels; its autobiographical content portrays the problems created by absolutism for an idealistic priest who questions abstractions and seeks fulfilment in freedom of conscience. O'Donovan's *Waiting* (1914) is also critical of papal views, in this case the *Ne Temere* decree. His modernism may seem mild to modern readers, as his style may seem somewhat dated, but his progressive, liberal views, tested in difficult circumstances, give his novels an impressive intensity.

Decidedly different in outlook was **Daniel Corkery** (1878-1964), whose plays were published as *The Yellow Bittern and Other Plays* (1920). He also wrote *The Threshold of Quiet* (1917), a novel which explored some provincial lives. His short stories are most interesting. The first collection of them, *A Munster Twilight* (1916), was based on life both in the Gaelic-speaking areas of west Cork and Cork city. Corkery was most at ease in what has been described as 'Puritanism and local self-satisfaction'. The stories of *The*

Hounds of Banba (1920), however, show him moving towards his deepest interest. In them a decidedly simplistic admiration for the guerrilla forces in Cork adversely affects his artistic sense; he was to be more at home when expressing a somewhat restrictive, *a priori* cultural nationalism. In *The Hidden Ireland* (1917) he evokes the social history within which 18th century Irish writers expressed their sense of an inherited Gaelic culture.

In *Synge and Anglo-Irish Literature* (1931) Corkery proclaimed the characteristics of an Irish outlook to be a preoccupation with religion, nationalism and the land. The stories in *The Stormy Hills* (1929) continue his earlier themes, but in the best of them, 'Carraig-an-Aifrinn', realism tempers an idealised concept of the land with an actuality of the envy and greed that it can promote. In *Earth out of Earth* (1939), his last collection of stories, Corkery returned to urban situations in a more urbane mood.

Some other writers of fiction who published before the First World War can be summed up fairly briefly. **Seumas O'Kelly** (1875-1918) wrote a melodramatic novel in *The Lady of Deer Park* (1917). The stories of *The Weaver's Grave* are his most lasting contribution. **Forrest Reid** (1875-1947) wrote fifteen books, among them a trilogy, dealing mainly with boyhood and adolescence, but his two autobiographical books *Apostate* (1926) and *Peter Waring* (1937) are most worth reading. **Eimar O'Duffy** (1893-1935), a revolutionary, disillusioned by the 1916 Rising, wrote possibly the first despairing record of the frustration it caused in *The Wasted Island* (1919); he is better known for his inventive irony in *King Goshawk and the Birds* (1926) in which he voiced his dislike of modern life.

JAMES STEPHENS

James Stephens (?1880-1959) is well-known for his frequently anthologised poems, such as 'The Red-Haired
Man's Wife' and 'The Goat Paths':

> I would think until I found
> Something I can never find,
> Something lying on the ground,
> In the bottom of my mind.

His versions of Irish poems notably those by **Daibhí Ó
Bruadáir** – 'A Glass of Beer' and 'Skim Milk', and from
Eoghán Ó Rathaille, including 'Egan O'Rahilly', are inter-
pretative. It is in his prose, however, that the quintessence
is found of a most original author on whose two books *The
Charwoman's Daughter* (1921) and *The Crock of Gold*
(1912) rest his main claim to fame. The first expresses the
anger Stephens felt at the social injustice that had created
Dublin's slums but it is also a highly whimsical account of
the relationship between the charwoman and her daughter,
aptly named Mary Makebelieve. *The Crock of Gold,* however, greatly in vogue in the 1920s, is much more impressive and more representative of its author's idiosyncratic
attitudes. Thus philosophical seriousness blends with
satiric parody of the pagan gods; Caitlin, after she has been
seduced by Pan, later chooses marriage to Angus Óg who
influences the logical Philosopher for the better. Like the
Thin Woman, the Philosopher has had a lot to learn; his
adventures provide some of the comedy and some serious
stimulus to thought. The variety of attitudes is balanced by
narrative skill and the final apocalypse, when the false
values of urban life are contrasted by the fairies with the
country of the gods, is superbly handled.

Though Stephens was to imbue other books, *The Demi-
Gods* (1914) and *Irish Fairy Tales* (1920), with his quirky,

puckish humour and to write two volumes of his versions of the *Táin Bó Cuailgne*, *The Crock of Gold* remains a one-off in its poetic imagination and invention. Stephens wrote excellent prose, which appears also in his sharply focused stories, collected in *Etched in Moonlight* (1928). He was a superb conversationalist and the quality of his talk, witty, wide-ranging, unexpected and nimble, is amazingly well-caught in the printed versions of his very successful radio talks *James, Seamus and Jacques* (1960).

6. THE LITERARY REVIVAL

WILLIAM BUTLER YEATS

W B Yeats was born in Dublin but spent much of his youth in London. His father, the artist **John Butler Yeats**, moved his family there in 1867, when Willie was an infant. In 1881, the family returned to Dublin, where Yeats attended the High School, then the School of Art. In 1887 the artist moved the family back to London again, where they were very short of money. Willie decided he wanted to be a poet and struggled to make a living by literary journalism.

Originally hoping to write poems like those of Allingham about Ballyshannon, he was attracted by the local legends and folklore of Sligo, where he had spent many childhood years. He then discovered exciting material in ancient Irish literature, having been introduced to translations of it by John O'Leary, an old Fenian who returned to Dublin after years of enforced exile in Paris. He also read Irish novelists such as William Carleton who made Ireland their subject matter. This was all new to him and offered a way to escape from the influence of English literary tradition. Allingham's *Poems* had appeared in 1888; the next year Yeats's long poem *The Wanderings of Oisin* marked the beginning of a new era in Irish literature.

In accordance with his theories, Yeats's poem brought together pagan and Christian elements in its story of Oisin, who spends 300 years with the fairy princess Niamh on three enchanted islands before returning to Ireland, meeting St Patrick and realising his own human mortality. The poem was influenced by pre-Raphaelitism and touched with melancholia but it brought into being new subject matter and a new beauty of style:

> Caoilte, and Conan, and Finn were there,
> When we followed a deer with our baying hounds,
> With Bran, Sceolan, and Lomair,
> And passing the Firbolgs' burial-mounds,
> Came to the cairn-heaped grassy hill
> Where passionate Maeve is stony-still;
> And found on the dove-grey edge of the sea
> A pearl-pale, high-born lady, who rode
> On a horse with bridle of findrinny;
> And like a sunset were her lips,
> A stormy sunset on doomed ships;
> A citron colour gloomed in her hair,
> But down to her feet white vesture flowed,
> And with the glimmering crimson glowed
> Of many a figured embroidery;
> And it was bound with a pearl-pale shell
> That wavered like the summer streams,
> As her soft bosom rose and fell.

Yeats's *The Celtic Twilight* was published in 1893 and was re-written for the 1902 edition with additional material collected in Co Galway with the aid of Lady Gregory, writings centring on the supernatural and based mainly on conversations with Sligo people. The collection contained a final poem 'The Celtic Twilight', a name often applied to much of the writing produced in the literary revival by Yeats and those whom he influenced and inspired. He himself thought that the first of his poems to contain the rhythm of his own music was 'The Lake Isle of Innisfree', written in 1888 and probably still the best-known of his poems.

When Charles Stewart Parnell, the leader of the Irish Parliamentary Party, died in 1891, Yeats realised that there was a general disillusion with and a lull in Irish political life, consequent upon the split in the Party which had resulted from Parnell's affair with Mrs O'Shea. He thought there was now a vacuum into which literary activity could be diverted. Yeats had been arguing the need for Irish people to realise their spiritual and cultural heritage, to develop a distinctive and distinguished literature based upon a fusion of Christian and pagan traditions. He launched two influential societies, the Irish Literary Society in London in 1891 (which still exists) and the National Literary Society in Dublin in 1892.

He wrote many articles and reviews to popularise the new Irish writing, insisting always upon the need to achieve the highest literary standards. He disliked what he considered the over-rhetorical clichés of the balladry earlier popularised in the patriotic pages of *The Nation*; he wanted Irish literature to escape the influence of English by exploring Gaelic mythology and legend as well as local traditions. He was well aware of the general European interest in Celticism, stimulated by the Ossianic tales James MacPherson had produced in the late 18th century and eventuating in the work of Ernest Renan (1823-92), the Breton philologist and historian, and in Matthew Arnold's *On the Study of Celtic Literature* (1867), which stressed the unique and neglected contribution of the imaginative Celtic race.

There was plenty of material to hand. Yeats regarded it as a marble block waiting almost untouched but emphasised the need to learn how to use a chisel. Young Irish writers became aware of the new dimensions offered by the past. Knowing no Irish himself, Yeats had been excited by Standish James O'Grady's (1846-1928) *History of Ireland: the Heroic Period* (1878) which he regarded as starting the revival. He was also influenced by Sir Samuel Ferguson and other poets and translators.

He set himself to read the work of those who had been encouraged by George Petrie, an excellent artist himself, who had gathered kindred spirits around him in the Ordnance Survey of the 1830s: they included such scholars as Eugene O'Curry, John O'Daly, and John O'Donovan. Their successors were James Henthorn Todd, Standish Hayes O'Grady, Whitley Stokes, Douglas Hyde, Eleanor Hull, who founded the Irish Texts Society, and Kuno Meyer, a German who founded a School of Irish Learning in Dublin in 1903. Some of Yeats's compilations, such as *Fairy and Folk Tales of the Irish Peasantry* (1888), *Irish Fairy Tales* (1892) and his selections from Irish novelists, followed up the work of these earlier scholars and gave the subject a wider, more general audience.

Yeats himself was soon established as a love poet. When he was twenty-three he fell in love with Maud Gonne, a year younger, a strikingly beautiful, tall, well-to-do girl who had decided to devote herself to the cause of Ireland's independence, seeing herself as a patriotic leader.

> The wrong of unshapely things is a wrong too great to be told;
> I hunger to build them anew and sit on a green knoll apart,
> With the earth and the sky and the water, re-made, like a casket of gold
> For my dreams of your image that blossoms a rose in the deeps of my heart.

An effective, indeed a rousing public speaker, and an effective journalist, she enjoyed the excitement of political activity. Yeats, desperately poor, could only offer her his poetic devotion, hoping one day this would be rewarded. In 'He Wishes for the Cloths of Heaven' he says that had he the heavens' embroidered cloths he would spread them under her feet:

> But I, being poor, have only my dreams;
> I have spread my dreams under your feet;
> Tread softly because you tread on my dreams.

He did, however, propose to her in 1891 and continued to do so for many years. The poetry he wrote her until he was thirty-five was defeatist, dreamy, sad and hauntingly beautiful. He associated Maud Gonne with Ireland in the Rose poems which contained Gaelic mythology but were related to the symbolism he had found in his occult studies (he was a member of the Order of the Golden Dawn, a magical society) and in his study of Blake (whom he edited), Swedenborg and Boehme. His friend Arthur Symons made him aware of the French symbolist poets and his writing, also influenced by Walter Pater, became more elaborate and more allusive, reaching a peak in *The Wind Among the Reeds* (1899).

Yeats and Middle-Age

Yeats did not remain permanently caught in the web of the shadowy, misty, dreamy twilight he had created. At the turn of the century, he said, everyone got down off their stilts. Disappointed in love and disillusioned with revolutionary nationalism, he and Maud Gonne had left the Irish Republican Brotherhood (IRB), precursor of the IRA, by 1900. His love poetry changed, for in 1903 Maud Gonne had married John MacBride, who was to be one of the fifteen men executed after the 1916 Rising. He recorded his feelings in an unpublished poem:

> My dear is angry, that of late
> I cry all base blood down
> As if she had not taught me hate
> By kisses to a clown.

His published poems now celebrate the love he had previously expressed for her. They are dignified and moving in their stark account of his vain courtship and in such poems as 'No Second Troy' she is elevated to the stature of Homer's Helen. His poetic techniques also changed. In his early adjectival poetry, he had excluded all that was not beautiful. Now verbs and nouns predominate as he strips off the Celtic decoration, substituting realism for romance in the often bitter, disillusioned poems of *The Green Helmet*, and permitting politics into the powerful poetry of *Responsibilities*, as in 'September 1913':

> Was it for this the wild geese spread
> The grey wings upon every tide;
> For this that all that blood was shed
> For this Edward Fitzgerald died,
> And Robert Emmet and Wolfe Tone,
> All that delirium of the brave?
> Romantic Ireland's dead and gone,
> It's with O'Leary in the grave.

Indeed, when his *Collected Poems* appeared in eight volumes in 1908, it seemed to many that his poetic inspiration had dried up. 'All things', he wrote, 'can tempt me from this craft of verse.' He had immersed himself in 'theatre business, management of men' to some effect and it is time to consider how the Abbey Theatre came into being.

The Irish Theatre

Yeats had written verse plays since his teens and his *The Land of Heart's Desire* was produced in London as a curtain-raiser for Shaw's *Arms and the Man* in 1894. He had always hankered for an Irish theatre but the possibility of creating one had seemed a mere dream until 1897. In that year, he was staying with Lady Gregory at her big house, Coole Park, in Co Galway, which was to become a centre where Irish writers were welcomed and where Yeats spent his summers in an orderly routine.

The widow of an Irish landlord and MP and former Governor of Ceylon, Lady Gregory began to see the failings of the landlord class in Ireland and was moving towards nationalism when she met Yeats. With a neighbour, Edward Martyn, she discussed the idea of an Irish theatre with Yeats and the three of them, with George Moore as producer, staged the first plays of the Irish Literary Theatre in 1899 at the Antient Court Rooms in Dublin. These were Yeats's *The Countess Cathleen*, a poetic play written for Maud Gonne, and Martyn's *The Heather Field*, an Ibsenite play. Yeats's play roused nationalist anger on the grounds that its story of a Countess sacrificing her soul to save her starving people seemed to portray Irish people selling their souls.

Other plays were produced in 1900 and 1901 and, after the performance of George Russell's *Deirdre* and Yeats's *Kathleen* (later *Cathleen*) *ni Houlihan*, with Maud Gonne in the title role, the National Theatre Society was formed in 1902 with Yeats as President. Maud Gonne's performances had a devastating effect, prompting Yeats to wonder in old age whether his play had stimulated young men into taking part in the 1916 Rising. The plays were performed by the Fay Brothers' dramatic company, Yeats approving their unusual acting technique. He sought simplicity in acting and plain scenery. His desire for heroic poetry was united with a wish, shared by Lady Gregory, who began to display great dramatic skills, to bring the speech of the countryside to city audiences.

The agreeable life at Coole Park, reinforced by a visit to Italy in 1907 where he admired the benefits of princely patronage on the arts of the Renaissance, gave Yeats an appreciation of an idealised art-nourishing aristocracy. He began to write a new kind of play, intended not for the Abbey but for small, select audiences and which were first played in London drawing-rooms. These plays were linked to the Japanese Noh theatre (though in plays such as *On Baile's Strand* and *Deirdre* Yeats was already moving towards Noh techniques before knowing anything about Noh and its conventions). He was introduced to the Noh by Ezra Pound who was editing Fenollosa's translations of Noh plays. This gave an impetus to Yeats's *Four Plays for Dancers* – though he was still writing plays suitable for the Abbey, such as *The Player Queen* (1919) with its highly original, strange humour and subject matter.

Yeats's Mature Achievement

Yeats's personal world changed again in 1916. Maud Gonne's husband, from whom she had been separated since 1905, was one of the leaders shot after the failure of the 1916 Rising, which was the subject of his great musing poem, 'Easter 1916'. Yeats went to France in 1916 to propose to her yet again, to be refused in the usual way. He next proposed to her daughter Iseult and when she refused him he married Georgie Hyde Lees in October 1917. They had known each other since 1911; she shared his interests in mysticism and spiritualism and after their marriage she began automatic writing. This provided material for his book *A Vision* and gave him the self-confidence out of which he wrote poems which conveyed his ideas of historical change and the decay and destruction of Western civilisation, using the symbols of the gyres, and the phases of the moon. Many poems centred upon the medieval tower near Coole, a potent symbol which he had bought for £35 in 1917 and which he and his wife restored as a summer residence. As several poems recount, he was there during the civil war which ensued after the Treaty of 1922 had brought the twenty-six county Irish Free State into existence. He records the civil war and the absence of accurate news about it reaching Coole in 'The Road at my Door':

> We are closed in, and the key is turned
> On our uncertainty; somewhere
> A man is killed, or a house burned,
> Yet no clear fact to be discerned:
> Come build in the empty house of the stare
> A barricade of stone or of wood
> Some fourteen days of civil war;
> Last night they trundled down the road
> That dead young soldier in his blood ...

Yeats received the Nobel Prize for Literature in 1923. (Two years later Shaw was also to be awarded it.) The poet whom some thought finished in 1908 was now demonstrating his power in *The Wild Swans at Coole* (1917), with its elegy 'In Memory of Major Robert Gregory' and 'An Irish Airman foresees his Death', while *Michael Robartes and the Dancer* (1920) showed him concerned with past, present and future, notably in that disturbingly prophetic poem 'The Second Coming':

> Things fall apart; the centre cannot hold
> Mere anarchy is loosed upon the world,
> The blood-dimmed tide is loosed, and everywhere

The ceremony of innocence is drowned;
The best lack all conviction, while the worst
Are full of passionate intensity.

The Tower (1928) and *The Winding Stair* (1933) bore witness to his continuing ability to blend the affirmative beauty of his early poetry and the often harsh disillusionment of his middle period into a richly colourful, emotive, allusive yet outspoken and challenging poetry, often obsessed with old age and the lack of certainties. The Ireland which was a microcosm of what was happening in the world at large had been well used and served by his predecessors, Swift, Berkeley, Goldsmith and Burke; his play about Swift, *The Words upon the Window-Pane*, (1934) showed that he could employ realism to achieve a paranormal effect.

Despite increasing ill-health he went on writing immensely vigorous poetry. After the Crazy Jane poems with their stress on sex came philosophical poems, celebratory poems about his dead friends. ('The Municipal Gallery Revisited'), and the magisterially questioning poems of old age such as 'What Then?', set in the farmhouse in the hills south of Dublin to which he moved in 1932. Other poems of his later years were 'The Gyres', 'Lapis Lazuli', 'The Circus Animals' Desertion', 'Under Ben Bulben' and that haunting poem 'The Man and the Echo' with its final admission of his particular truth, that he could not know whether there was a future life, for knowledge of which he had searched throughout his own life:

> O Rocky Voice,
> Shall we in that great night rejoice?
> What do we know but that we face
> One another in this place?
> But hush, for I have lost the theme,

Its joy or night seem but a dream;
Up there some hawk or owl has struck,
Dropping out of sky or rock,
A stricken rabbit is crying out,
And its cry distracts my thought.

LADY GREGORY

Lady Augusta Gregory (1852-1932) is coming to be appreciated more these days for her own achievement. For many years she seemed the stern charwoman of the Irish theatre, the severe handmaiden-patron of Yeats, the authoritative grande dame of Coole Park in Co Galway. Now the identification of her passionate love poems to Wilfrid Blunt, the knowledge of her affair with John Quinn and especially the publication of her diaries and letters reveal other sides of her valiant, amusing personality and the nature of her more than supportive role is more fully understood.

Her own writing is excellent. In *Cúchulain of Muirthemne* (1902) she translated the tales of the Ulster cycle; in *Gods and Fighting Men* (1904) the tales of the mythological and Finn cycles. These she told in lively narrative using the Hiberno-English spoken in Kiltartan, a farmland near Coole. She omitted some of the violence and sexuality of the originals but conveyed their vigour and strength, as in her treatment of the story called 'The Championship of Ulster' in which Cúchulain is the only Ulster hero to meet the challenge of a churl who dares anyone cut off his head on condition that he can do the same to the challenger next day. Cúchulain beheads him and the next day the challenger appears and tells Cúchulain to put his head on the block. He does so, and Lady Gregory tells the story with narrative skill:

But when the axe came down, it was with its blunt side, and it was the floor it struck, so that Cúchulain was not touched at all. And all the chief men of Ulster were standing looking on, and they saw on the moment that it was no strange clown was in it, but Curoi, son of Daire, that had come to try the heroes through his enchantments.

'Rise up, Cúchulain,' he said. 'Of all the heroes of Ulster, whatever may be their daring, there is not one to compare with you in courage and in bravery and in truth. The Championship of the heroes of Ireland is yours from this out, and the Champion's Portion with it, and to your wife the first place among all the women of Ulster. And whoever tries to put himself before you after this,' he said, 'I swear by the oath my people swear by, his own life will be in danger.'

With that he left them.

She helped Yeats greatly with the dialogue of *Cathleen ni Houlihan*, *The Pot of Broth* and *Where There is Nothing*. Many of her own plays exhibit a fine sense of comedy. Some of them concentrate upon historical events; these include *The Deliverer* (1911) and *Grania* (1911). A play she wrote with Douglas Hyde, *The Rising of the Moon* (1907) and her own *Dervorgilla* (1907) are examples of her strongly-held nationalist views.

Her translations from the Irish in *The Kiltartan Poetry Book* (1918) and the vigorous folklore of *Visions and Beliefs in the West of Ireland* (2 vols, 1920), collected over many years in collaboration with Yeats, are a valuable work of preservation and presentation.

She played a crucial role in the literary revival: she could think straight and had a vigour that achieved much. Modest in self-assessment, she had impressive creative energy which she put to the service of making the rapidly declining Gaelic cultural tradition available not only to the Kiltartan people, for whom she conceived herself writing, but for wider audiences ever since. With Yeats's praise of her in mind it is well worth reading her autobiography *Seventy Years* (1974).

JOHN MILLINGTON SYNGE

A different use was made of peasant speech and idiom by **John Millington Synge** (1871-1909), whose first play *In the Shadow of the Glen* (1903) caused trouble with nationalists, including Maud Gonne. It is an archetypal tale of old husband and young wife in which Nora, the wife, decides to opt for the life of the tramp:

> 'But you've a fine bit of talk, stranger, and it's with yourself I'll go.'

It was followed by *Riders to the Sea* (1904), the tragedy of an old island woman who has lost her husband and five sons to the sea and in vain begs her last son not to sail to the mainland on what turns out to be a fatal voyage. Maurya's last words remind us that there is a constant battle between man and the elements; the play ends on a note of classical strength and simplicity:

> 'No man at all can be living for ever, and we must all be satisfied.'

In 1904 the nascent Irish theatre received a great boost. Annie Horniman, an Englishwoman who shared Yeats's occult interests, bought the old Mechanics Institute theatre (which included a former morgue) in Abbey Street, Dublin. It was opened as the Abbey Theatre in 1904. Miss Horniman paid a subvention which converted the amateur actors to professionals and Yeats, Lady Gregory and Synge became directors.

A crisis in the new theatre's affairs came quickly. Synge,

Above: Jonathan Swift
(1667-1745)

Right: Maria Edgeworth
(1767-1849)

Oscar Wilde (1854-1900)

George Bernard Shaw (1856-1950)

William Butler Yeats (1865-1939)

James Joyce (1882-1941)

Samuel Beckett (1906-1989)

Right: Kate O'Brien
(1897-1974)

Below: Brian Friel (b1929)

Seamus Heaney (b1939)

who had learned his Irish at Trinity College and then studied music and literature abroad, had made several visits to the Aran Isles between 1898 and 1902, writing *The Aran Islands* (1907) in 1901 and following it with *In Wicklow and West Kerry* (1911). Out of his knowledge of Irish and the English spoken in rural areas he constructed his own kind of Hiberno-English, an energetic language, imaginative, poetic and evocative, in which he wrote plays that convey the exuberance and stoicism he found among country people, expecially in the Aran Islands, then a wild and largely unvisited area, and in the remoter parts of Co Wicklow which he reached by bicycle.

He transformed this material into the powerful drama of *The Playboy of the Western World*, his own tough poetic mind shaping the classical kind of comedy, with its contrast between romanticism and reality, into a tragi-comic mode that seems particularly Irish in its tensions and contradictions. The play caused riots in the theatre at its first performances, nationalists regarding it as a libel on Irish peasant life, rejecting the subtleties inherent in the character of the playboy Christy Mahon (who declares he'll go romancing through a romping lifetime), and ignoring the play's high seriousness in the midst of the fantasies created by and around Christy. For instance, Pegeen Mike can be lyrical:

> ... It's little you'll think if my love's a poacher's, or an earl's itself, when you'll feel my two hands stretched around you, and I squeezing kisses on your puckered lips, till I'd feel a kind of pity for the Lord God is all ages sitting lonesome in His golden chair.

But her tragedy is to lose him, 'the only playboy of the western world'.

Yeats fought courageously and successfully on behalf of the play. He evinced largeness of mind in committing himself so deeply to working for a theatre (he was its general manager until 1910) in which his poetic heroic plays interpreting Irish mythology in his own terms – *On Baile's Strand* (1905), for instance, his treatment of the death of the Irish hero Cúchulain, and *Deirdre* (1907), the tragic legend of 'one woman and two men', the quarrel which has no mending – were not so successful as those of the realistic dramatists.

OTHER DRAMATISTS

Those whose work was produced during Yeats's managership included **William Boyle** whose best plays were *The Building Fund* (1905), a study of avarice, *The Eloquent Dempsey* (1906), a farcical treatment of political trickery, and *The Mineral Workers* (1906) which contrasted the go-ahead ideas of a returned emigrant engineer with the conservation of the local country folk.

Padraic Colum (1881-1972), novelist and poet as well as dramatist, was author of the controversial anti-recruitment play *The Saxon Shillin'*: he went on to write several other successful plays, *The Land, Broken Girl* and *Thomas Muskerry*, which conveys the petty nature of life as well as the greed which emerges in a small country town. **T C Murray** (1873-1959), one of that group of playwrights labelled collectively the 'Cork realists', wrote a sombre play in *Birthright*, in which love of the land leads to fratricide; his *Autumn Fire* was a later study of frustration.

In *The Country Dressmaker* **George Fitzmaurice** (1878-1963) blended comedy and realism, this neatly-made play dealing with a woman refusing a local suitor and eventually marrying her former lover who returns as a widower after ten years in America. A man of original mind, Fitzmaurice wrote seventeen plays in all, a certain bitterness being alleviated by inventiveness, his realism tempered by fantasy.

The best of these realists was **Lennox Robinson** (1886-1958) , who became manager of the theatre in 1910. His plays are inevitably well-made, *The Clancy Name* being the first of his realistic plays about life in Cork. The range of his drama was extended by treatment of politics, of Emmet and Parnell, but he found his true metier in comedy, *The Whiteheaded Boy* and *Drama at Inish* having an admirable lightness and sureness of touch.

A different subject for realistic treatment was provided by the sectarian politics of Ulster, the tribal warfare of its dogmatically divided streets. This was given suitably tough dramatic treatment in *Mixed Marriage* by **St John Ervine** (1883-1971), a Belfastman whose *Boyd's Shop* is a good example of his later work which embraces the clash of youth and age and explores the tragic effects of intolerance.

DOUGLAS HYDE

The year that Yeats published *The Wanderings of Oisin*, 1889, saw another book emerge which testified to its author's skills and sensibilities. **Douglas Hyde** (1860-1949) in *Leabhar Sgealuigheachta* produced a collection of stories and riddles in Irish which he had obtained from living speakers, some of which he included with his translations of them in *Beside the Fire* (1890). His use of Hiberno-English is stimulating, his material reminding readers of the oral nature of folk tales. He had published his own original poems in Irish using the pen-name *An Craoibhín Aoibhinn* ('the Pleasant Little Branch'). An earlier plea for the Irish language was followed up when he gave his inaugural address as the first president of the Irish National Literary

Society founded by Yeats whom he had earlier met in Dublin at the Young Ireland Society. Entitled *The Necessity for de-Anglicising Ireland* it was very influential.

Hyde and Yeats had similar aims though their routes were different. Hyde was the first President of the Gaelic League, founded in 1893 (he resigned in 1915 when it became too political) with the purpose of keeping the Irish language spoken in Ireland. Some of the League's organisers came from the Gaelic Athletic Association (GAA), founded in 1884 to promote traditional Irish games.

In 1938 Hyde became the first President of Ireland. The excellent Hiberno-English translations in his *Love Songs of Connacht* (1893) and his *Religious Songs of Connacht* (1905-6) were informed by his Gaelic scholarship, at its most authoritative in *The Story of Early Gaelic Literature* (1895) and *A Literary History of Ireland* (1899). His play *Casadh an tSúgáin*, based upon Yeats's scenario and later translated by Lady Gregory as *The Twisting of the Rope*, was produced by the Irish Literary Theatre in 1891 and was welcomed as a contribution to the literary revival. Here is one of his translations from the Irish:

> For thee I shall not die,
> Woman high of fame and name,
> Foolish men thou mayest slay,
> I and they are not the same.
>
> Why should I expire
> For the fire of any eye,
> Slender waist or swanlike limb,
> Is't for them that I should die?
>
> The round breasts, the fresh skin,
> Cheeks crimson, hair like silk to touch,
> Indeed, indeed, I shall not die,
> Please God, not I, for any such!

The golden locks, the forehead thin,
The quiet mien, the gracious ease,
The rounded heel, the languid tone,
Fools alone find death from these.

Thy sharp wit, thy perfect calm,
Thy thin palm like foam of the sea;
Thy white neck, thy blue eye,
I shall not die for thee.

Woman, graceful as the swan,
A wise man did rear me, too,
Little palm, white neck, bright eye,
I shall not die for you.

OTHER WRITERS OF THE LITERARY MOVEMENT

Other Irish poets writing in the 1890s were dwarfed by
Yeats. One of the most impressive of them was his friend
the idiosyncratic **George Russell** (1867-1935) who saw
visions and painted them. He wrote and painted under the
name 'AE', his *Homeward, Songs by the Way* (1894) followed by other volumes. He also wrote plays and made a
considerable contribution to Irish life not only by his work
for the Irish Co-operative Society but by his skilled and hos-
pitable editing of the *Irish Homestead* from 1895 and the
Irish Statesman from 1923. Two other friends of Yeats
who wrote a number of memorable poems were **T W
Rolleston**, known for 'The Dead at Clonmacnoise' and for
his co-editing, with Stopford Brooke, the *Treasury of Irish
Poetry* (1900) and the prolific **Katharine Tynan**
(1861-1931) whose *Louise de la Vallière* (1885) proved
popular. This was followed by seventeen other volumes,
her early poems often tinged with sadness were well
crafted and she also wrote over a hundred novels.

There were many other writers: **Jane Barlow**, who
wrote narrative poems and slow-moving novels; **Alice**

Milligan (a minor poet) who shared editing the *Shan Van Vocht* with **Ethna Carbery** (Anne Isabel Johnston) who wrote stories and poems: **Dora Sigerson Shorter** who tinged her poems, fairy, folk and religious, with melancholia: **Susan Mitchell,** known for pungent wit, her poems supplying a satiric view of members of Dublin's literary society.

The misty melancholia persisted into the twentieth century in the poems of **Eva Gore-Booth**, **Nora Hopper**, **Alice Furlong**, **Mary Devenport O'Neill** and, the most prominent, **Seumas O'Sullivan** (James Sullivan Starkey, 1879-1958), now best known for his essays and constructive editing of *The Dublin Magazine* from 1923 to 1958.

7. THE ABBEY IN THE 1920s AND 1930s

SEAN O'CASEY

Yeats had returned to Ireland for good in 1922 and acquired 82 Merrion Square, a Georgian townhouse in the centre of Dublin. He was himself in the middle of several activities of the new Irish state, for he had become a senator and, as his speeches show, took his position very seriously. He was still involved in the work of the Abbey, which gained fresh vitality with the discovery of a very different kind of playwright, **Sean O'Casey** (1880-1964).

O'Casey began work as a labourer at the age of fourteen, was involved in various parish charitable activities, took to socialism and joined several organisations, including the Gaelic League and the Irish Transport and General Workers Union (ITGWU), becoming Secretary of the Irish Citizen Army. He left this organisation in 1914 but wrote its history later. The first of his plays to be produced by the Abbey, in 1923, was *The Shadow of a Gunman*, which debunked the reputation of the IRA's gunmen:

SEUMAS: It's the civilians that suffer; when there's an ambush they don't know where to run. Shot in the back to save the British Empire, an' shot in the breast to save the soul of Ireland. I'm a Nationalist meself, right enough – a Nationalist right enough, but all the same – I'm a Nationalist right enough – I believe in the freedom of Ireland, an' that England has no right to be here, but I draw the line when I hear the gunmen blowin' about dyin' for the people, when it's the people that are dyin' for the gunmen! With all due respect to the gunmen, I don't want them to die for me.'

Juno and the Paycock proved the most successful of the Abbey's plays so far staged, running for a second week and winning O'Casey the Hawthornden Prize. This play's action takes place in the period of the Civil War; it concerns itself with the price the stoical women pay for the vain heroics of the men. Juno's courage is contrasted with the drunken irresponsibility of the Paycock, her boasting, lying husband 'Captain' Boyle and his parasite companion Joxer Daly. The drunken entrance of the Paycock is arresting and excellent theatre:

> ... I'm telling you ... Joxer ... th' whole worl's ... in a terr ... ible state o'... chassis!'

The two men are wonderfully achieved comic creations, for the lightness of laughter evoked in the richly inventive, arrestingly vigorous English spoken so spontaneously in the Dublin slums gives the play the complexity of tragicomedy. This makes its dark, inexorable ending, the 'terrible state o' chassis' that ensues with the reversal of apparent good fortune the more moving. The masculine vanity and fecklessness of violent or would-be violent men, the inhumanity of absolute abstractions, set against the true bravery of non-combatants, mainly patient women, was a theme that occupied O'Casey. Juno Boyle receives the news of her son's death with a fortitude that reminds us of another brave woman, Maurya, in Synge's *Riders to the Sea*:

> MARY: Oh, it's thrue, it's thrue what Jerry Devine says – there isn't a God, there isn't a God; if there was He wouldn't let these things happen!
>
> MRS BOYLE: Mary, Mary, you mustn't say them things. We'll want all the help we can get from God an' His Blessed Mother now! These things have nothin' to do with the Will o' God. Ah, what can God do agen the stupidity o' men!

His next play, *The Plough and the Stars*, is set in the brief period of the 1916 Rising. It, too, gains its dramatic force from the use of contrast, in this case differences between the realities of violence and the platitudes of patriotic rhetoric which demanded it. This provocative challenging of what had become orthodox views about the Rising proved too much for the Dublin audiences of the 1920s, too close to the events of the Rising, the Anglo-Irish War and the Civil War to appreciate O'Casey's dramatic achievement. Yeats defended him vigorously, again braving the anger of the Abbey audiences when they rioted against the play, telling them:

> You have disgraced yourselves again. Is this to be an ever recurring celebration of the arrival of Irish genius? Synge first and then O'Casey.

O'Casey moved to voluntary exile in England, the first play he wrote there, *The Silver Tassie* (1929), being rejected by the Abbey. It was an anti-war play, a result of O'Casey's experimental movement toward expressionism; it lacked the exuberant dramatic energy of his Dublin plays. There followed *Within the Gates* (1933), a play about social injustice, and *The Star Turns Red* (1940), an attempt to blend Christianity and Marxism; both extended O'Casey's adventuring into expressionism, as did *Red Roses for Me* (1942), *Purple Dust* (1945) and *Oak Leaves and Lavender* (1948). Something of his earlier exuberance surfaced again in *Purple Dust* where the workmen are trying to sell hens to Poges:

1ST WORKMAN [*persuasively – towards Poges's paper*]: Listen, here, sir; if it's genuine poulthry you want, that lay with pride an' animation, an' not poor, insignificant fowls that set about th' business o' layin' like a member o' Dolye Eireann makin' his maiden speech, I have a sthrain o' pullets that'll give you eggs as if you were gettin' them be steam!

POGES [*angrily – glancing over the top of his paper*]: Go away, go away, man, and don't be driving me mad!

3RD WORKMAN [*towards Poges's paper*]: Oh, the lies that some can tell to gain their own ends! Sure, sir, everyone knows that his poor hins are harmless; only venturin' to lay when heavy thunder frightens them into a hasty sign o' life! But it's meself can give you what you want, with a few lively cocks thrown in, to help them on with the work of furnishing nourishment to the whole world.

Then came plays dealing critically and satirically with Ireland: *Cock-a-Doodle Dandy* (1949), *The Bishop's Bonfire* (1955), *The Drums of Father Ned* (1959) and *Behind Green Curtains* (1961).

These experimental plays were not successful, and O'Casey's later return to Irish subject matter lacked the immediacy of his first three plays. He took up the writing of autobiography with gusto. The first two of his six volumes, *I Knock at the Door* (1939) and *Pictures in the Hallway* (1942) contain somewhat self-conscious writing but their account of his early life in the Dublin slums is evocative whereas the other volumes now seem over-written and at times unduly querulous. Only at their best moments can these autobiographies carry off their allusiveness, their punning, their parodies and their grievances. O'Casey's reputation, however, rests secure. The creative tension and scintillating use of Dublin speech of his three first plays, *The Shadow of a Gunman, Juno and the Paycock* and *The Plough and the Stars*, their ironic portrayal of contradictions between the boastful apparently heroic glamour of the revolutionaries and the reality, the outcome of their violence, made him a major dramatist, not just of his own time.

Much of the drama staged in the Abbey after the row over O'Casey's *The Plough and the Stars* in 1926 was not very distinguished. **George Shiels** (1886-1949) proved popular with comedies that sought and got easy laughter, his *Grogan and the Ferret* (1933) typical of this genre. *The Rugged Path* (1940), however, is more critical of the contemporary scene, in a study of rural murder. **Paul Vincent Carroll** (1900-68) wrote stronger plays, *Shadow and Substance* (1937) centring on a clash between a schoolmaster and a canon; this clash of characters was repeated in another of his plays, *The White Steed* (1939).

DENIS JOHNSTON

An exception to the general run of Irish dramatists in this period was **Denis Johnston** (1901-1984). A well-educated barrister, he wrote in *The Old Lady Says No!* a brilliantly clever, expressionist critique of Irish nationalism contrasting Robert Emmet's past idealism with the actuality of life in the contemporary Irish Free State. The title of the play was taken from a remark written on the script referring to Lady Gregory, when it was returned to the author, to be subsequently produced at the Gate Theatre in 1929.

Johnston based *The Moon on the Yellow River* (1931) upon a struggle between republicans and Free Staters which results in the destruction of a power station. Tausch, a German, stresses the benefits electric power can bring to Ireland (we remember that the Shannon Scheme of the 1920s which harnessed the power of the Shannon to provide electric power was built by the German firm of Siemens Schukert) but he is given a mock warning (this play to a certain extent sends up melodrama) by Dobelle:

> Here we have bogey men, fierce and terrible bogey men, who breathe fire from their nostrils and vanish in the smoke.
>
> TAUSCH: You have what?
>
> DOBELLE: And we have vampires in shimmering black that feed on blood and bear bombs instead of brats. And enormous fat crows that will never rest until they have pecked out your eyes and left you blind and dumb with terror.
>
> TAUSCH: Come, come, Mr Dobelle.
>
> DOBELLE: And in the mists that creep down from the mountains you will meet monsters that glare back at you with your own face.

A Bride for the Unicorn (1933) was over-complex but *Blind Man's Buff* (1936), a play about a murder trial which exposes the shortcomings of the legal system, was rewritten into the more successful *Strange Occurrence on Ireland's Eye* (1956). Johnston's concern with the pressure of the state upon individuals was stressed in *The Golden Cuckoo* (1939). *The Dreaming Dust* (1940) seizes upon what he thought were Jonathan Swift's predicaments, a masque-like play which was followed by a biographical study *In Search of Swift* (1959) which produced new evidence and theories about Swift's birth and his relationships with Stella and Vanessa.

Johnston used his expressionism to work out his own ideas by analysing a variety of those held by others: he wanted, Shaw-like, to provoke his audiences into taking a fresh look at crucial issues of morality. *The Scythe and the Saint* (1958), set in the Easter Rising, is an intellectual reaction to O'Casey's *The Plough and the Stars*, shaped no doubt by Johnston's own experiences as a war correspondent, so well told in *Nine Rivers from Jordan* (1953).

8. JOYCE AND FICTION: 1920s–1940s

JAMES JOYCE

The Irish literary renaissance, in the creation of which Yeats had played such a leading role, might well be considered over by 1922, the year the Irish Free State came into being. New talents had been emerging before then, the major figure among them **James Joyce** (1882-1941). He grew up in Dublin, the family impoverished by the feckless conviviality of his father. Joyce went to Clongowes Wood College and subsequently to Belvedere, both Jesuit schools, and then to University College, Dublin. After he graduated he had two brief spells in Paris, returning after his mother, a devout Catholic (and pregnant fifteen times), died of cancer in 1903. A schoolmaster for a time, he was briefly a guest of Oliver St John Gogarty in the Martello tower at Sandycove, south of Dublin. In October 1904 he eloped with Nora Barnacle; they lived in Pola, then in Trieste, where Joyce taught English, returning only briefly to Dublin in 1909 and 1912. He and his family spent the First World War in Zurich, moving to Paris in 1920. They left Paris for Vichy early in the Second World War and later settled in Zurich where Joyce died in 1941.

Joyce wrote lyric and conventional love poems, thirty-six of them, published in *Chamber Music* (1910), reflecting his deep interest in musical effects; the thirteen poems of

Pomes Penyeach (1926) have been set to music by many distinguished composers.

It is for his prose, however, that Joyce is celebrated. He chose Dublin for the scene of the fifteen stories of *Dubliners* (1914) 'because that city seemed to me the centre of paralysis'. The characters in these stories illustrate childhood, adolescence, maturity and public life. They are written in what he called 'a style of scrupulous meanness' in which the narration, and dialogue in Dublin speech, the nuances and tones of which were so accurately captured by Joyce, intermingle as individuals': lives are demonstrably dominated by frustration, inertia, poverty, alcoholism and the conformity encouraged by the Catholic Church. In *Dubliners* Joyce is not only realistic, casting an ironic eye on sordid situations, but he also deploys symbolism and impressionism and links the stories together thematically.

The last story, 'The Dead', is, however, more complex in its social comedy and its examination of the character of Gabriel, whose superiority is shaken by his realising how little he knows of his wife. In it Joyce, like Maturin before him, stresses the differences between the west and the east of Ireland, regarding the Shannon as a boundary:

> The time had come for him to set out on his journey westward. Yes, the newspapers were right: snow was general all over Ireland. It was falling on every part of the dark central plain, on the treeless hills, falling softly upon the Bog of Allen and, farther westward, softly falling into the dark mutinous Shannon waves.

An autobiographical novel, the surviving part of which was posthumously published in 1944 as *Stephen Hero*, illustrated Joyce's radical, questioning attitudes as a young man, his rejection of Dublin and the values he imputed to it. Despite many excellent and some very amusing passages in it, it was in many ways immature, and Joyce, realising this, abandoned it and applied a stricter aesthetic and architectonic control to the more condensed autobiographically based novel published in 1918 as *A Portrait of the Artist as a Young Man,*

In this novel we follow Stephen from infancy to the independence that he seeks by 'silence, exile and cunning'. He escapes from the pressures of family, political and religious life in Ireland. The five divisions of the book cover the awakening of his consciousness: the Parnellite controversy at home; bullying at school from boys and standing up to the bullying Father Dolan; then scholarship and sex; these all followed by the Retreat with its famous hell-fire sermon which turns him back to devotion, though he then decides against the priesthood and shapes his aesthetic experience – an encounter with a girl on the seashore provides an epiphany, the 'day of dappled seaborne clouds' – into a philosophy of self-realisation shaped by his Catholic upbringing and his awareness of Aristotle and Aquinas.

Stephen is young and wilful and wildhearted, alone 'amid a waste of wild air and brackish waters'; a girl stood before him, alone and still, gazing out to sea; and Stephen is touched by the wonder of mortal beauty.

> ... and when she felt his presence and the worship of his eyes her eyes turned to him in quiet sufferance of his gaze, without shame or wantonness. Long, long she suffered his gaze and then quietly withdrew her eyes from his and bent them towards the stream, gently stirring the water with her foot hither and thither. The first faint noise of gently moving water broke the silence, low and faint and whispering, faint as the bells of sleep; hither and thither, hither and thither; and a faint flame trembled on her cheek.
>
> Heavenly God! cried Stephen's soul, in an outburst of profane joy.

His is the vocation of the artist, as we learn from the diary entries that conclude the book, when the artist goes 'to encounter for the millionth time the reality of experience and to forge in the smithy of my soul the uncreated conscience of my race.'

Ulysses was published in 1922, a year of successful experiments in modern literature in which there were also published T S Eliot's *The Waste Land* and Yeats's *Later Poems*, Virginia Woolf's *Jacob's Room*, and D H Lawrence's *Aaron's Rod*. Joyce modelled his novel upon the structure of Homer's *Odyssey*, various episodes of which are parodied. The action, however, is concentrated into the events of eighteen hours in Dublin on 16 June 1904. These eighteen episodes centre upon Leopold Bloom, a Jewish advertising canvasser, his wife Mollie and Stephen Dedalus: these unheroic characters are modern equivalents of Ulysses, Penelope and Telemachus.

The novel is highly experimental. Joyce blends acute, detailed observation of Dublin and its life with what he called interior monologues (the stream of consciousness) and dialogues; the subconscious thoughts of the characters are also conveyed. He employs literary parody and a variety of literary forms, as, for instance, in the brothel scene, where the Circe episode takes the form of a surrealist drama. This technique gives the novel an impersonal quality. Joyce had learned from Homer the need for variety, and so the substance as well as the style varies, conveying the rich difference between various people and their outlooks.

Ulysses, then, provides a picture of modern urban life. Bloom, a cuckold, is no heroic Ulysses, but he is kindly and endowed with humour, his mind is eclectic and his attitudes tolerant. His character is set against the fixed attitudes of nationalism, racial hatred and male domination:

I stand for the reform of municipal morals and the plain ten commandments. New worlds for old. Union of all, jew, moslem and gentile. Three acres and a cow for all children of nature. Saloon motor hearses. Compulsory manual labour for all. All parks open to the public day and night. Electric dishscrubbers. Tuberculosis, lunacy, war and mendicancy must now cease. General amnesty, weekly carnival, with masked licence, bonuses for all, esperanto the universal brotherhood. No more patriotism of barspongers and dropsical imposters. Free money, free love and a free lay church in a free lay state.

Bloom's adulterous wife Mollie conveys in a soliloquy her memories of past love affairs and her earthy, sensual attitude to sex. Stephen Dedalus, back from Paris, rejects the mysticism deployed by writers in the literary revival, highly conscious of differences between what he sees and feels. He also rejects both family and religion in the Circe episode when he is haunted by a vision of his pious mother. He can be regarded as being in search of a spiritual father just as Bloom is in search of a son.

Joyce borrowed the structure of classical epic to impose structural order upon his view of the flux of experience, upon his inventive power of story telling, upon his sense of symbolism. There are many parallels to the *Odyssey* in characters and episodes (The 'Citizen', for instance, hurling a biscuit tin at Bloom parallels Polyphemus hurling rocks at Ulysses and his men).

Finnegans Wake (1939) was seventeen years in the making, progress hindered by Joyce's failing sight. It seemed to him his most significant work. It is the record of a night; the mind of the sleeping HCE (HC Earwicker) is interpreted, the punning in many languages and the stream of consciousness carrying allusions to mythology and religion, to all the vast amount of learning at Joyce's command.

There are many guide books to the dream world of Finnegans Wake and while guidance is certainly helpful, the
book can be enjoyed if it is simply read aloud – especially if
its local Dublin life is followed and fathomed. Here is the
light-hearted beginning of the Ondt and the Gracehoper:

> Let us here consider the casus, my dear little cousis
> (hussenhasstencaffincoffintussemtossemdamandamnaso
> aghcusaghhobixhatouxpeswchbechoscashlcarcarcaract)
> of the Ondt and the Gracehoper.
>
> The Gracehoper was always jigging ajog, hoppy on
> akkant of his joyicity, (he had a partner pair of findlestilts
> to supplant him), or, if not, he was always making
> ungraceful overtures to Floh and Luse and Bienie and Ves-
> patilla to play pupa-pupa and pulicy-pulicy, and langten-
> nas and pushpygyddyum and to commence insects with
> him, there mouthparts to his orefice and his gambills to
> there airy processes, even if only in chaste, ameng the
> everlistings, behold a waspering pot. He would of curse
> melissciously, by his fore feelhers, flexors, contractors,
> depressors and extensors, lamely, harry me, marry me,
> bury me, bind me, till she was puce for shame and allso
> fourmish her in Spinner's housery at the earthsbest schop-
> pinhour so summery as his cottage, which was cald four-
> millierly Tingsomingenting, groped up.

This is a comic epic on a grand scale, often cryptic, often
humorous as it follows the concerns of the Earwicker
family. Humphrey Chimpden Earwicker, Anna Livia
Plurabelle, the sons Shem and Shaun and Issy the daughter. These personae are representations, on one level, of
aspects of Dublin, of male and female, the universals rep-
resented in the philology – the general accretion being
arrived at conveying universality, an interpretation and
shaping of the particular continuity of the contemporary
world, and at the consideration of creation in general.

Irish Novelists Writing in England

JOYCE CARY

Though **Joyce Cary** was some six years younger than Joyce (he was born in 1888 and died in 1957) his first novel did not appear until 1932. He had had, therefore, ample time to develop his ideas and distil his experiences. Born in Derry, he spent holidays from his English schools at his grandmother's house on the Inishowen peninsula in Co Donegal. An art student in Paris and Edinburgh, he then went to Oxford where he got a fourth class degree. He served with the Red Cross in Montenegro in the Balkan War in 1912-13, then worked in the Nigerian political service until 1920, serving in the Cameroons from 1915 to 1916. In 1920 he settled in Oxford for life.

In the twelve years before *Aissa Saved* was published in 1932 Cary had contemplated basic issues of human life, especially those raised by his experience of the clash between the Christianity of the colonists and the local religion of pagans, between colonialism and tribalism. *Aissa Saved* was the first of four novels set in Africa, the best of them *Mister Johnson* (1939).

Castle Corner (1938) brought together his varied interests: in it he shows an Anglo-Irish family affected by the processes of history. Here are fine pictures of Donegal life blended with Irish and African experiences and an awareness of how English life, too, was changing. Very different were the subjects of *Charley is my Darling* (1946) and *A House of Children* (1941), the one a study of delinquent evacuee children in Devon and Cornwall, the other idyllic yet clear-eyed in descriptions of timeless childhood holidays in Donegal, written in a limpidly creative prose, reminiscent at times of the capacity for lyricism evinced by

James Joyce whose work Joyce Cary greatly admired:

> We travelled through this enormous and magnificent scene
> in tranquil happiness ... and the memory of bathing, shout-
> ing, tea, the blue smoke of picnic fires, was mixed with the
> dark evening clouds shaped like flying geese, the tall water
> stretching up to the top of the world, the mountains sinking
> into darkness like whales into the ocean and over all a sky so
> deep that the stars, faint green sparks, seemed lost in it and
> the very sense of it made the heart light and proud, like a
> bird.

The scope of Tolstoy and Dostoevsky is apparent in his two
trilogies about English life. In the first, *Herself Surprised*
(1941), *To Be a Pilgrim* (1942) and *The Horse's Mouth*
(1944), Cary was affected by Blake, especially in his artist
character Gully Jimpson, an archetypal bohemian, Sara
Monday being a blend of temptress and mother figure
while Wilsher is a classic image of conservatism. After he
had dealt with the generation gap in *The Moonlight* (1946)
and with the courage of a woman in *A Fearful Joy* (1949),
Cary wrote his second trilogy, *Prisoner of Grace* (1952),
Except the Lord (1953) and *Not Honour More* (1953), now
placing individuals in a setting in which political, economic, and, especially, social values were shifting. He had
learned the art of conveying thoughts and attitudes and the
endless rewriting of his earlier days had borne fruit in the
easy flow of his later novels. His non-fiction is persuasive,
notably in *Power in Men* (1939) and *Selected Essays* (1976).

C S LEWIS

Surprised by Joy (1955), the autobiography of **C S Lewis**
(1898-1963), has many parallels with Louis MacNeice's *The
Strings are False* (1965): both northerners had stepmothers;
both had to suffer English schools; both subsequently

became university teachers in England. Lewis, however, remained one all his life, first at Oxford, then at Cambridge. A distinguished medievalist, his *Allegory of Love* (1936) gained him a considerable reputation. But he was also a writer of science fiction with *Out of the Silent Planet* (1938), *Perelandra* (1943) and *That Hideous Strength* (1945), a sinister picture of organisations at work. He also wrote allegorical children's stories, the Narnia Chronicles. He appeared as a modern Christian apologist in *The Problem of Pain* (1940) and *The Screwtape Letters* (1942), advice from an older devil to a younger about tempting sinners. These books proved very popular and Lewis followed them with others on Christianity and human love.

ELIZABETH BOWEN

The family of **Elizabeth Bowen** (1899-1973), like that of Joyce Cary, had come to Ireland in the 17th century. She inherited the family's big house Bowen's Court in Co Cork, in 1930 and wrote about it in *Bowen's Court* (1942) eventually selling it in 1959, finding it impossible to run on her own after her husband's death in 1952. Her youthful years in Dublin are described with precision in *Seven Winters* (1942), a little-known book:

All here stood for stability. The front doors were, as I say, fresh-painted – crimson, chocolate, chestnut, ink-blue or olive-green. One barrister friend of my father's had a chalk-white front door I found beautiful. And each door – to this my memory finds no single exception – bore its polished brass place. Daughter of a professional neighbourhood, I took this brass plate announcing its owner's name to be the *sine qua non* of any gentleman's house. Just as the tombstone says '*Here Lies*' the plate on the front door (in my view) said '*Here Lives*'. Failure to write one's name on one's door seemed to me the admission of nonentity.

The householder with the anonymous door must resign himself to being overlooked by the world – to being passed by by the postman, unfed by tradesmen, guestless, unsought by friends – and his family dwelt in the shadow of this disgrace.

The Last September (1929), with its convincing portrait of a young girl's romantic love affair broken up by a powerful older woman, is an atmospheric evocation of an Anglo-Irish big house during a period of political tension; the undertones of the impending 'troubles' are well evoked.

In general, Elizabeth Bowen's fiction was not innovative in style. She seemed at ease within established literary conventions and liked to explore social nuances, herself treading a path between respectability – often to be rated as snobbishness – and a farouche quality sometimes, perhaps surprisingly, verging on vulgarity, *The Death of the Heart* (1938) being a good example of this. *The Heat of the Day* (1949) convincingly renders the tensions and excitements of war-time London, in this case the unfolding of a story of spying and counter-measures; it is probably her best novel, as 'The Demon Lover' is her best short story, given strength by her own belief in the supernatural. Her stories are collected in several volumes, the last, *A Day in the Dark*, appearing in 1965.

World of Love (1955) returned to Ireland, to a classic theme: a big house in decay and the effect of this situation upon its inhabitants. While she employed her often simple style very effectively in her fiction to reveal what was covered by socially respectable exteriors (the range ran from innocence and fearfulness to brutal betrayal and masterful manipulation) her later autobiographical writing, notably her unfinished *Pictures and Conversations* (1975), benefitted from the sense of spaciousness she deployed in that form. However romantic at times her fiction could be, she maintained a sense of detachment in retailing it, whereas her personal preferences and attitudes prevail more obviously in her writing about history, travel and literature, as this passage from *Pictures and Conversations* indicates:

> Becoming a writer knocked a good deal of nonsense out of my system ... As a novelist, I cannot occupy myself with 'characters', or at any rate central ones, who lack panache, in one or another sense, who would be incapable of a major action or a major passion, or who have not at least a touch of the ambiguity, the ultimate unaccountability, the enlarging mistiness of personages 'in history'. History, as more austerely I now know it, is not romantic. But I am ... If you began in Ireland, Ireland remains the norm: like it or not ...

Censorship in the Free State

The Irish Free State in the 1920s and 1930s was not sympathetic to artists' exploration and experimentation. A highly conservative Catholic orthodoxy prevailed in the new state. Symptomatic of official attitudes was the Censorship of Publications Act passed in 1929, which proved to be a highly contentious measure and one of the reasons for the setting up of the Irish Academy of Letters as a vehicle of protest against what was, in effect, an attempt to exclude from Ireland writing which questioned Catholic orthodoxy on such matters as sex and contraception. (An Appeal Board was created in 1949 which lessened the absurdities and restrictiveness of the Board of Censors; the virtual abolition of the Act came about in 1967 when another bill allowed for the unbanning of books after twelve years.)

Obviously, censorship prevented Irish writers from open discussion of social issues and many of them sought their living abroad. Opposition to realistic presentation of Irish life was, of course, not confined to official channels. The kind of resentment which had been stirred up against Yeats's, Synge's and O'Casey's plays surfaced on a local plane on the publication of Brinsley MacNamara's (John Weldon, 1890-1963) forthright portrayal of the midland village to which he had returned after five years in the United States in *The Valley of the Squinting Windows* (1918). The book was burned and MacNamara then moved to Dublin, writing various plays for the Abbey and other outspoken novels.

LIAM O'FLAHERTY

Similar castigatory exposure of diverse standards of peasant life, 'pagan' and 'civilised', in the Aran Islands in the early novels of **Liam O'Flaherty** (1896-1984) gained force from a potent mixture of realism and romance, a force developed further in the depressing darkness of *The Informer* (1925), *Mr Gilhooley* (1926) and *The Assassin* (1928).

In 1930 O'Flaherty wrote *A Tourist's Guide to Ireland*. Priests, politicians and publicans were now seen as the oppressors of the peasantry, his understanding of whom had appeared in the short stories which he wrote in Irish as well as English. His collection of Irish stories was published in 1953 in *Dúil*.

O'Flaherty, born on Inishmore in the Aran Islands, had given up studies for the priesthood, organised a corps of republican volunteers but then joined the Irish Guards, being seriously wounded in 1917. In the Civil War he joined the republicans, later taking up communism. He shed his 'isms' when he went to London after the Civil War, and became preoccupied with self-exploration in the thirties, a

period when he suffered a series of breakdowns. His autobiographies record the sense of frustration this engendered
in him.

Skerrett (1932) again explored Aran material, this time
portraying a school-teacher who, when thrown out by the
parish priest, turned reformer, then revolutionary, and
finally lost his reason. In this novel and the very powerful
Famine (1937), based upon his knowledge of Aran famines
and folklore as well as of history, O'Flaherty wrote his most
impressive fiction. The genre of the short story, however,
proved an effective curb on his tendency to excessive
expressionism and to preaching on the general predica-
ment in his novels. Indeed compassion surfaced here
rather than the violence or the irascibility which so marked
his earlier work. All his fiction expresses a turbulent energy.
His best-known story, 'Going into Exile', for instance, conveys the force of the emotions that father and son suppress:

> They stood in silence fully five minutes. Each hungered to
> embrace the other, to try to beat the air, to scream with
> excess of sorrow. But they stood silent and sombre, like
> nature about them hugging their woes.

KATE O'BRIEN

Kate O'Brien (1897-1974), born in Limerick, herself the
product of a wealthy middle-class Catholic family, portrayed the rise of a family like her own in the 19th century
through three generations in a discursive novel, *Without
my Cloak* (1931), which won the Hawthornden Prize. But
Mary Lavelle (1936), was banned. It was the story of an Irish
girl growing into adulthood in Spain and choosing to con-
summate her love.

The Land of Spices (1941) was banned also, an objection
being raised to a sentence when Helen Archer finds her

homosexual father and his male pupil Etienne 'in the embrace of love'. This novel tells of how a nun, Mère Marie Hélene Archer, comes to realise how she became a nun, to forgive her father and to begin to be able to love again: that love enables her to fight on behalf of a young girl so that she can take up a scholarship and go on to the university. The novel is feminist in its reasonable appreciation of women's needs for careers – in the church as well as outside it – and in the cooperation of women with each other.

Small wonder that Kate O'Brien wrote another novel, *The Last of Summer* (1943) to offer apparently detailed comment on what she saw as the illiberal and complacent Puritanism of post-Treaty Ireland. She had discussed the condition of Ireland earlier in *Pray for the Wanderer* (1938), a response to the earlier banning of *Mary Lavelle,* an argument for the use of individual judgement. Her character Matt Costello was drawn as highly courageous, his greatest faith a belief in personal liberty that drove him out of the Church but made it impossible for him 'to find any resting place in contemporary life'. His friend Tom Mahoney attacks contemporary religiosity and hypocrisy in savage terms:

> Religiosity is becoming a job in this country, you might say. A plank. A threat and a menace. A power in the land, in fact, my boy! In the Island of Saints and Scholars! Yah – it's disgusting! It's a matter of municipal policy now wearing this little button and that little badge, holding a banner here and running to make a retreat there, with Father O'Hegarty warning you kindly about this, and Father O'Hartigan rapping you over the knuckles about that and Father O'Hanigan running off to the bishop to talk about you! Town Council stuff! Pure jobbery. 'But is he a good practising Catholic, Father O'Dea?' 'And are you sure he leads a moral life, Sister Mary Joseph?' And if you aren't sure, will you kindly make it your life-work to

find out! My God, it's terrible! We need an Ibsen here, Matt.

O'Brien's novels portray heroines caught between potentialities and the chances of achieving them, in search of love and, ultimately, freedom. Ana, Princess of Eboli, the heroine of *That Lady* (1946), probably Kate O'Brien's best novel, is at the mercy of Philip II of Spain; the book shows what losses a woman of great distinction, of a proud independence of spirit, can incur in her pursuit of freedom.

SEÁN O FAOLÁIN

Seán O Faoláin (John Whelan, 1900-1991) grew up in Cork where he was influenced by Daniel Corkery against whose narrow nationalistic views he later rebelled. In the Civil War he fought as a republican but became disillusioned. After taking degrees, in University College, Cork and Harvard, and teaching in England, he returned to Ireland in 1933. *Vive Moi* (1964) is a splendid autobiographical account of this early period.

O Faoláin's stories in *Midsummer Night Madness and other Stories* (1932) and a subsequent series of historical novels – *Bird Alone* (1936) is the best of them – explore tensions between individuals and trace the progress of revolutionary hopes into subsequent conservatism. The short story form suited him better than the novel and his three volumes of *Collected Stories* (1980-82) are a fine achievement. He knew his craft and wrote illuminatingly about it in *The Short Story* (1948). 'The Faithless Wife' is a good example of his craft and probably his most ironic and witty. It tells of a foreign diplomat who falls for an Irish married woman and is surprised that she turns out to be not all calm, cool elegance when she arrives in what she called the 'beddaroom'.

The Bell

After volumes published in 1937 and 1948 which recorded his dislike of the repressive climate of Irish Catholicism, O Faoláin gradually developed a detached attitude to Ireland in his stories, keeping his criticisms of the pervasively puritanical climate for his editorials in *The Bell*, a journal which he founded and edited from 1940 to 1946. The journal was influential in its condemnation of Irish authoritarianism, its questioning of literary criticism (such as that of Daniel Corkery) based on what O Faoláin regarded as out-of-date nationalist views. He had little sympathy with the rationale behind the state of Ireland outlined in de Valera's constitution of 1937. One of his editorials, for example, analysed the position of the contemporary Irish writer:

> This struggle between the inescapable Past and the insistent Present, between luxuriating into nostalgia and working out of ambition, has made itself felt strongly since 1916. If there is any distinct cleavage among us to-day it is between those who feel that tradition can explain everything, and those who think it can explain nothing ... We are living ... to a great extent experimentally, and must go on doing so.

The Bell provided a lively forum for the intellectual discussion of matters of public interest. The editorship passed from O Faoláin to **Peadar O'Donnell** (1893-1986) whose guidance of the journal from 1946 to 1954 inevitably imposed some of his strong left-wing views on it. These had informed several of his books including *Islander* (1927) and *Adrigoole* (1929), *There will be Another Day* (1963) and *Proud Island* (1975).

As O Faoláin's criticism of the state hardened, his general view of humanity grew mellower (if more ironic) and his sense of humour was more in evidence. He became very skilled in evoking the atmosphere of a scene, and he could impart his reflections on life, and particularly on the importance of individuality, in a convincing conversational style. The short story required suggestion combined with compression, he thought, and he could now convey compassion economically in stories such as 'Two of a Kind'.

O Faoláin wrote several biographies – of Eamon de Valera, Constance Markievicz, Cardinal Newman, Daniel O'Connell and Hugh O'Neill – and travel books, all of which are marked by characteristic easy eloquence.

FRANK O'CONNOR and MICHAEL MCLAVERTY

Another Corkman influenced by Daniel Corkery, also a republican in the Civil War, **Frank O'Connor** (Michael O'Donovan, 1903-66), wrote an engaging autobiography of his childhood in *An Only Child* (1962). His short stories record how romantic illusion was jarred by the realities, the brutalities of guerrilla war, the title story in *Guests of the Nation* (1931) being a haunting account of the reprisal murder of two hostages. In his stories O'Connor took great pains to create the effect of a good conversationalist talking, the narration consequently flowing naturally and yet with detachment.

He was, however, far from detached himself when he contemplated his contemporary Ireland, where he, too, fought against the repression experienced by young people in provincial life. *The Wild Bird's Nest* (1932) contained translations from the Irish, and in the same year his novel *The Saint and Mary Kate* was published. He wrote plays for the Abbey, and gave up his librarianship to become a full-time writer and broadcaster in 1939.

Much of his work was banned in Ireland. A novel *Dutch Interior* (1940) which deals with the frustration of young people in Cork, his translation of Brian Merriman's *Cúirt an Mheán-Oíche*, a late 18th century long Irish poem dealing with sexual repression and the celibacy of the clergy in a comic, celebratory, bawdy way, published as *The Midnight Court* (1945), the short stories of *The Common Chord* (1947) and *Traveller's Samples* (1951) found a more appreciative reception in England and especially America, where the New Yorker valued his short stories.

He also found enthusiastic audiences (he later lectured superbly) in his academic teaching in various colleges and universities in the United States, and this work led to two books of criticism, *The Mirror in the Roadway* (1956), a stimulating study of the novel, and *The Backward Look* (1967), an immensely readable if eclectic history of Irish literature, and to two books of translations from the Irish, *Kings, Lords and Commons* (1959) and *A Golden Treasury of Irish Poetry,* 600-1200 (1959), co-edited with David Greene. O'Connor's feeling for the spirit of his originals led him to write translations which are accurate, lively and moving. Here is a portion of his version of the anonymous Irish poem 'Kilcash' (the seat of a branch of the Butler family), it laments the decline of a once powerful household:

> My grief and my affliction
> Your gates are taken away,
> Your avenue needs attention,
> Goats in the garden stray.
>
> The courtyard's filled with water
> And the great Earls where are they?
> The Earls, the lady, the people
> Beaten into the clay.

Michael McLaverty (1907-1992) is very much a Northern writer who began his career with short stories marked by a spareness in style. His *Collected Short Stories* appeared in

1978. His novel *Call My Brother Back* (1939) and its successor *Lost Fields* (1941) hark back to his childhood while *In This Thy Day* (1945) he emphasised the tensions of rural life in Ulster, contemplating the problems of ordinary people, their situations conveyed in simple and highly effective prose. His subsequent novels continued to deal with conflicts of good and evil in the same unadorned but telling way.

FRANCIS STUART and MOLLY KEANE

Two writers born within the first five years of the 20th century have had rebirths in renewed public perception of their talents. **Francis Stuart** (b 1902), whose first marriage in 1920 was to Maud Gonne's daughter Iseult, was involved in the Civil War on the Republican side and was interned until 1923. He was praised for his early novels, especially *Pigeon Irish* (1932) and *The Coloured Dome* (1932) which are romantic in their creation of individual outcasts who oppose current mediocrity: they suffer from not suffering martyrdom and gain some insight as a result. But the early promise seemed to vanish and of his subsequent novels *The White Hair* (1936) is probably the most coherent.

When Stuart, who had gone to Germany to lecture in 1939 and give radio talks from 1942-44, emerged after various vicissitudes, including imprisonment until 1946, he stayed in Freiburg until 1949. He wrote three novels there, *The Pillar of Cloud* (1948), *Redemption* (1949) and *The Flowering Cross* (1950). In these the main characters, who have seen the effects of war and subsequent social collapse, gain some optimism from their associations with women who have also suffered from the horror of war, but can achieve forgiveness.

Other novels of lesser achievement followed and it was

not until the publication of *Blacklist, Section H* in 1971 that Stuart achieved success. This was his first piece of faction which blended autobiography with fiction in a powerful, direct way, avoiding the elusive romantic mysticism of his previous fiction. Without it he would probably have faded into the recesses of literary history. The originality and honesty of approach of this book gave Stuart the confidence to express himself freely in further, more experimental, novels in which he blends religion and sex and shapes his material into relative coherence. The protagonist is the artist who explores freely whatever the outcome, a dissenter by nature, idiosyncratic insofar as this allows him to achieve absolute freedom. No wonder the book ends as it does:

> Whatever it was at the other end there was no way of telling. It might be a howl of final despair or the profound silence might be broken by certain words, that he didn't yet know how to listen for.

Molly Keane (1905-96) came as a pleasant surprise to younger readers when her *Good Behaviour* (1981), followed by *Time after Time* (1983), presented the Anglo-Irish in shabby, faded grandeur, in situations of black comedy, out of touch with the Ireland in which they live precariously, bills unread and unpaid. These are novels written with precise control, showing the perennial conflict between children and parents in a closed world of hunting, shooting, fishing, dancing and drinking. The underlying cruelty is there, explored in a scalpel-sharp analysis of the social comedy, so reminiscent of Somerville and Ross in *The Real Charlotte*. So we have a son at public school and university, a daughter whose future is marriage (but who is there to marry her?), a landlord father sleeping with a servant, a mother who is a painter and very self-centredly detached, all presented in the objective dead-pan narrative found in Somerville and Ross with a nice use of current phraseology deployed at crucial moments. *Loving and Giving* (1988) is yet another picture of a decaying big house, this one framing a woman's memories. Older readers already knew Molly Keane's earlier work which was written under the name **MJ Farrell**: eleven novels, the best of them the outspoken *Devoted Ladies* (1934), and five plays that were very successful, *Spring Meeting* (1938), the liveliest of them.

MICHAEL FARRELL

Another novel slightly out of its time warp was written by a contemporary of Elizabeth Bowen, **Michael Farrell** (1899-1962), *Thy Tears Might Cease* (1963) being published posthumously. It deals in part with a boy's growing up and his subsequent efforts to create a cultural conscience in the midst of revolutionary activity in the Black and Tan war. Farrell found it impossible to finish his work and it was excellently edited by **Monk Gibbon** (1876-87), himself the author of novels dealing with a schoolmaster's love affairs and of *The Seals* (1935), a haunting account of a seal hunt in the West of Ireland which deals with human cruelty.

MERVYN WALL and FLANN O'BRIEN

Written by a civil servant **Mervyn Wall** (**Eugene Welply**, b 1908), a Dubliner educated at University College, Dublin, *The Unfortunate Fursey* (1946) is a solemnly written account of the wildly funny story of a medieval brother and his relationship with the Devil, a joyous burlesque mocking puritanism and the church. The Devil strikes a bargin at the Synod of Cashel: he will rid Ireland of the 'hideous sin' of sex if the hierarchy ignores the others, 'simony, nepotism, drunkenness, perjury and murder'.

In *The Return of Fursey* (1948), there is satiric treatment of the censorship in the description of a medieval censor checking the library, burning many treasured manuscripts, Christian and pagan as well as four copies of the Old Testament which he denounces as being 'in general tendency indecent' (a phrase used by the Censorship in the Free State):

> One of his principal qualifications for the post of Censor was that each of his eyes moved independently of the other, a quality most useful in the detection of hidden meanings. Sometimes one eye would stop at a word which might reasonably be suspected of being improper, while the other eye would read on through the whole paragraph before stopping and travelling backwards along the way it had come, until the battery of both eyes was brought to bear on the suspect word. Few words, unless their consciences were absolutely clear, could stand up to such scrutiny.

Wall's *Leaves for the Burning* (1953) is a sardonic picture of Irish life before the 1960s; it was followed by two novels written in the same vein, *No Trophies Raise* (1956) and *Hermitage* (1962).

Joyce's delight in words and capacity for stylistic experimentation continued in the novels of **Flann O'Brien** (**Brian O'Nolan**, 1911-66; who also wrote as Myles na gCopaleen, the name taken from a character in Griffin's *The Collegians*, developed in Dion Boucicault's adaptation of that novel as *The Colleen Bawn). At Swim-Two-Birds* (1939) is a series of Chinese boxes: a Dublin student who is writing a book about an author, some of whose characters bring him to trial for mistreating them. This novel satirises sentimental treatment of Gaelic culture but uses material from Westerns and folk tales, its medieval Irish material counterpointing the contemporary student's life, its modernism, parody, pastiche, and exuberant absurdity making it a comic and compelling delight.

O'Brien's next novel, *The Third Policeman*, written in 1940, appeared posthumously in 1967; it is a disturbing novel in which the intellectual theories of de Selby, an eccentric philosopher, throw light on a state of fear. It questions the value of the imagination and O'Brien's own imagination is let loose upon Sergeant Pluck's theory that the nature of bicycles and riders interpenetrate, upon Constable McCruiskeen's box-making and the third policeman's control over a box that generates eternity. The narrative is part of the after-life, a fact that supplies a nihilistic basis to this mysterious story.

The Hard Life (1961) continues the study of futility and the grotesque, the squalor and vulgarity of the characters, the two brothers Manus and Finbarr, Mr Collopy and Father Kurt Fahrt, offset by the outrageous comic humour. *The Dalkey Archive* (1964) re-introduces de Selby, planning to destroy the human race, it satirises Joyce as a publican wanting to become a Jesuit and denouncing the works attributed to him, and shows Mick Shaughnessy trying to involve them in a complex piece of writing, the whole book developing doubts about the workings of imagination.

An Béal Bocht: nó An Milleánach (1941), translated as *The Poor Mouth: A Bad Story about the Poor Life* (1973) is an hilariously comic piece of black humour which satirises not only autobiographies set in the Gaeltacht (Irish-speaking districts in Ireland, described here as wet, poor and putrid) but also academics who patronise the native speakers of Irish.

O'Brien was at his best in his role as free-ranging satirist, his 'Cruiskeen Lawn' column, which ran from 1940 to 1966 in the *Irish Times*, being a magnificent coruscation of inventive wit, puns, parodies and punchlines in which the author castigated misuse of language (Irish and English) by bureaucrats and cranks, using the idioms of Dublin speech for anecdotes, conversation and comment, banal, cynical, dead-pan or else wildly exaggerated. Some examples of the column are contained in *The Best of Myles* (1985) and can be strongly recommended.

Regional Topics

SAM HANNA BELL and MARY LAVIN

Another writer to treat the rigours of life in remote areas was Sam Hanna Bell (1909-1990), himself a forceful novelist with his *December Bride* (1951) portraying the harsh unforgiving nature of a rural community in Northern Ireland. He lived in Belfast and worked for BBC Northern Ireland. He was deeply interested in Ulster's folklore and customs, an interest which emerges in the background of his later historical novels *A Man Flourishing* (1973) and *Across the Narrow Sea* (1979). Among other works he has written a very useful history, *The Theatre in Ulster* (1972).

Mary Lavin (1912-1996), on the other hand, dealt with life in small towns. She gained reclame with her first volume of stories *Tales from Bective Bridge* (1943), and later volumes, notably *The Becker Wives* (1946), increased her reputation further. She published regularly in the *New Yorker*, and the first of her two novels, *The House in Clew Street* (1945), is a good account of the provincial life from which a young man escapes by leaving his aunt's house and running off with a servant girl. Mary Lavin's short stories can seem rambling, without plot, but they convey the nature of her characters well as they face up to the problems of living: their speech, their occasional monologues, their moments of revelation add up to a very effective form of fiction.

9. POETRY AFTER YEATS

AUSTIN CLARKE

While alive Yeats had overshadowed other Irish poets; after his death he continued to do so, and some critics searched for a successor. At first this seemed to be **Austin Clarke** (1896-1974). *The Vengeance of Fionn* (1917), *The Sword of the West* (1921) and *The Cattle Drive in Connaught* (1925), however, had seemed dated; it looked as if Clarke had missed the bus by lingering too long in the Celtic Twilight, though he was developing an individual poetic vitality in these three volumes. In his mid-career during which he spent about fifteen years in London earning a living by book-reviewing, Clarke honed his stylistic skills, influenced by the complex techniques of Irish poetry, especially assonance. He became interested in the medieval monastic period, when the asceticism of the church was opposed to pagan sensuality. This interest appeared in three of his novels and is the basis of *Pilgrimage and Other Poems* (1928), while in *Night and Morning* (1938) faith and reason are in conflict, notably in the best poem he had written so far, 'The Straying Student' (who has been sent back from Salamanca):

> They say I was sent back from Salamanca
> And failed in logic, but I wrote her praise
> Nine times upon a college wall in France.
> She laid her hand at darkfall on my page
> That I might read the heavens in a glance
> And I knew every star the Moors had named.
>
> Awake or in my sleep, I have no peace now,
> Before the ball is struck, my breath has gone,
> And yet I tremble lest she may deceive me

And leave me in this land, where every woman's son
Must carry his own coffin and believe,
In dread, all that the clergy teach the young.

The tense poems of this volume reflect Clarke's personal problems, guilt still at odds with the rational approach he had adopted.

Clarke returned to Ireland in 1937 and he and Robert Farren founded the Dublin Verse Speaking Society (1940) and the Lyric Theatre (1944). In some plays of the early 1940s Clarke began to develop a stronger sense of satire; this side of his character emerged somewhat late in his poetry but may have been the more effective for that. *Ancient Lights* (1935) contained the fiercely indignant poem 'Martha Blake at fifty-one', while other poems attacked the repression of life in Dublin. Clarke's sense of sensuality seems to have been sharpened into more direct utterance by his satire, though at times the penalty is an over-emphasis upon the merely exotic, and he began to enjoy being outspoken in the somewhat freer climate of the 1960s. His own character is explained well in the first, frank volume of his autobiography *Twice Round the Black Church* (1962). A sense of sin, particularly the sin of sex, had been virtually built into him in youth. Jesuit-taught, as Joyce had been, he suffered similarly from having an excessively pious mother. Now, however, he felt free to attack Catholicism.

Later Poems (1961), followed by *Flight to Africa* (1963), led to the uninhibited and disturbing account of his experiences as a young man in a mental asylum in *Mnemosyne Lay in Dust* (1966). Franker still, the poems of *Tiresias* (1971) are part of his continuing defiance of censorious conservatism. 'The Healing of Mis' demonstrates how far he felt able to free a predilection for the near-pornographic.

The result of this late flowering is the expression of an unusual, somewhat sly, geniality. How much he enjoyed delivering a somewhat risqué address from the pulpit of St Patrick's Cathedral on the occasion of the Swift Tercentenary in 1967! *A Sermon on Swift* followed in 1968. He had come a long way now from the narrative of the 'Celtic' *The Vengeance of Fionn*, from his early technically impressive use of Gaelic material, through a good deal of self-torture into the sweeping ease of the variety of poetry he achieved in such satiric poems as 'Burial of a President', and those of immediate, local interest dealing with the trade in horses and the burning of an orphanage.

OLIVER ST JOHN GOGARTY

It was probably because of his dislike of the Celtic Twilight poets who continued to imitate his early style that Yeats did not include Austin Clarke in the Oxford Book of Modern Verse 1892-1935 (1936), though he approved enough of several of his juniors – Joseph Campbell, Padraic Colum and James Stephens – to include them. In this anthology he also placed many poems by **Oliver St John Gogarty** (1878-1957), a fellow senator, an ear, nose and throat specialist who wrote elegant lyrics on places and people with an easy grace. The title poem of *An Offering of Swans* (1923) tells of his releasing swans upon the river Liffey to celebrate his escape from gunmen, who had kidnapped him as a hostage in the Civil War, by plunging into the flooded river. Many of his amusing bawdy poems remain unpublished but his Rabelaisian wit informs 'On first looking through Kraft Ebbing's Psychopathia Sexualis', a parody of Keats's 'On First Looking into Chapman's Homer', and 'Ringsend' (then an insalubrious part of Dublin):

I will live in Ringsend
With a red-headed whore,
And the fan-light gone in
Where it lights the hall-door;
And listen each night
For her querulous shout,
As at last she streels in
And the pubs empty out.
To soothe that wild breast
With my old-fangled songs,
Till she feels it redressed
From inordinate wrongs,
Imagined, outrageous,
Preposterous wrongs
Till peace at last comes,
Shall be all I will do,
Where the little lamp blooms
Like a rose in the stew;
And up the back-garden
The sound comes to me
Of the lapsing, unsoilable,
Whispering sea.

His autobiographical books – the best are *As I Was Going Down Sackville Street* (1937) and *Tumbling in the Hay* (1939), a piece of autobiography disguised as the rumbustious account of medical students' lives at the turn of the century – are written with an insouciance and irreverence that matches George Moore's *Hail and Farewell*.

Country Poets

PATRICK KAVANAGH and FRANCIS LEDWIDGE

Reaction against the complexity of contemporary intellectualised poetry in the 1930s prepared a ready reception for the early poetry written on moral subjects by **Patrick**

Kavanagh (1904-1967) in *Ploughman and Other Poems* (1936). This was to a slight degree reminiscent of the earlier Keatsian lyricism of **Francis Ledwidge** (1887-1917) a road-ganger in Co Meath who founded the local group of Volunteers and was later killed at Ypres. He was befriended and encouraged by **Lord Dunsany** (1878-1957), an eccentric Meath landowner, himself a playwright and author of the Jorkens tales, creator of a mythological world in such volumes as *A Book of Wonder* (1912). Ledwidge possessed a melancholic sensibility well expressed in his lament for Thomas MacDonagh and in 'The Dead Kings'. Kavanagh, who lived on a small farm in Co. Monaghan until 1939 was, however, of tougher poetic fibre as poems such as the often quoted 'Shancoduff' and 'Spraying the Potatoes' were to demonstrate.

Kavanagh reacted strongly against both the romantic trappings of the Celtic ethos of the literary revival and the fashionable subject of the peasant. (Has it PQ? [peasant quality] – was reputed to be the first question asked about any play submitted to the Abbey from the 1920s to the 1940s). He attracted support because of this. *The Great Hunger* (1942) was a bitter, antipastoral poem lamenting the barren routine of bachelors, sexually frustrated, but married to the land, the 'clay' that dominates the poem's imagery. Kavanagh, who knew it well, disliked the rural kind of life that de Valera hoped to insulate within the Irish Free State.

This attitude permeated his *Tarry Flynn* (1948), a much more sombre book than his early autobiography *The Green Fool* (1938). Its realism clashes with the dream.

Tarry gazed across the valley right across to the plains of Louth, and gazing he dreamed into the past. O the thrilling daisies in the sun-baked hoof-tracks. O the wonder of the dry clay. O the mystery of Eternity ... the heavy slumbrous time and place made him forget the sting of the thorn of a dream in his heart. Why should a man want to climb out of this anonymous happiness in the conscious day.

He himself claimed the novel was nearer the truth than his autobiography, stating, acutely enough, that something uncertain must inevitably arise when a writer of fiction grapples with fact and becomes unsure of what is reality:

I've been telling lies all my life. I invented so many stories about myself in *The Green Fool* to illustrate my own unique character that I don't know myself what's true about me and what isn't.

When Kavanagh moved to Dublin he lived a fairly hand-to-mouth existence as an increasingly bad-tempered journalist, his poetry becoming savagely satiric and bitter. 'Who Killed James Joyce?' and 'The Paddiad' are examples of this strain. He had no mythology to support him and *A Soul for Sale* (1947) indicates his deep sense of personal disappointment: he had a heavy chip on his shoulder about being less well-educated than some people he despised. After the collapse of his journal *Kavanagh's Weekly*, the loss of a libel action and the onset of lung cancer, his outlook changed. His poetry switched in the 1950s, becoming less national in scope, less self-consciously aware of the past or of cultural aims, concentrating now on the significance of small, local events.

In this poetic rebirth he wrote some fine poems in *Come Dance with Kitty Stobling* (1960), full of a fresh appreciation of life and of natural beauty – notably in the sonnets on the Grand Canal, among them 'Canal Bank Walk':

O unworn world enrapture me, encapture me in a web
Of fabulous grass and eternal voices by a beech,

Feed the gaping need of my senses, give me ad lib
To pray unselfconsciously with overflowing speech
For this soul needs to be honoured with a new dress
   woven
From green and blue things and arguments that cannot
   be proven.

He learned to take himself more casually and his newly-found capacity for casual, indeed carefree, observation is decidedly impressive. His volume of *Collected Poems* (1964) was followed by *Collected Pruse [Prose]* (1967) while his posthumously published *Lough Derg* (1971) was written out of the angry view of Irish Catholicism he pursued in the 1940s.

Two Intellectual Poets

BRIAN COFFEY and DENIS DEVLIN

Very different from Kavanagh and Ledwidge in their approach were two highly intellectual poets, brought up in Dublin, who collaborated in a joint volume, *Poems* (1930). The elder, **Brian Coffey** (1905-1993), turned from research in science to philosophy and was a pupil of Jacques Maritain; he taught in London, Missouri and then in London again. Coffey found European neo-Thomist Catholicism satisfying as his long and cryptic poem *Advent* shows. He experimented with symbolism and surrealist techniques akin at times to those of Claudel. His intellectual rigour is challenging but decidedly difficult; he was a good translator of Mallarmé, Eluard and Neruda; his own *Selected Poems* were published in 1971. His friend **Denis Devlin** (1908-1959), influenced by the philosophy of Montaigne and the poetry of Eluard, moved from lecturing at University College, Dublin, to the Department of External Affairs

where his very successful career was cut short by leukae-
mia. Coffey edited his *Poems* (1964) and *The Heavenly For-
eigner* (1967).

Devlin, as avant-garde as Coffey, was also influenced by
French writers, especially Eluard whom he translated, as well
as Baudelaire and St John Perse. His *Lough Derg and Other
Poems* (1946) reveals his religious attitude to life. Cosmopolitan, well aware of the complexities of modern life (particularly for thoughtful Christians), his metaphysical mind could
be over-abstract at times but, like Coffey, he was a thinker
who assumed readers would share his philosophical or theo-
logical interests and interpret them.

Northern Poets

LOUIS MACNEICE, JOHN HEWITT and W R RODGERS

Three years after Kavanagh's birth in 1904, two very different poets were born in Ulster, both deeply affected by different kinds of northern childhoods. **Louis MacNeice**
(1907-1963) grew up in Carrickfergus, Co Antrim, where his
father was rector:

> ... born in Belfast between the mountain and the gantries
> To the hooting of lost sirens and the clang of trams:
> Thence to Smoky Carrick in County Antrim
> Where the bottle-neck harbour collects the mud which
> jams
>
> The little boats beneath the Norman castle,
> The pier shining with lumps of crystal salt;
> The Scotch Quarter was a line of residential houses
> But the Irish Quarter was a slum for the blind and halt ...

Despite schooling in England and reading classics at
Oxford before teaching the subject at the University of

Birmingham, despite being one of the left-wing English poets of the 1930s and a member of the BBC staff in London from 1941 on, the Irish element in his work cannot be ignored, for MacNeice cast a sharp eye on the Irish scene, as the five poems of *The Closing Album* (1939) reveal. Despite his very apparent dislike of the world of Irish politics he could respond to the countryside and to the individualism and personal mythologies that his own earlier attitudes had avoided in their emphasis upon the realities of modern urban life. Parts of *Autumn Journal* are highly critical of absolutes as he saw them in Irish politics:

Why do we like being Irish? Partly because
It gives us a hold on the sentimental English
As members of a world that never was,
Baptised with fairy water;
And partly because Ireland is small enough
To be still thought of with a family feeling,
And because the waves are rough
That split her from a more commercial culture;
And because one feels that here at least one can
Do local work which is not at the world's mercy
And that on this tiny stage with luck a man
Might see the end of one particular action.
It is self-deception of course;
There is no immunity in this island either;
A cart that is drawn by somebody else's horse
And carrying goods to somebody else's market.
The bombs in the turnip sack, the sniper from the roof,
Griffith, Connolly, Collins, where have they brought us?
Ourselves alone! Let the round tower stand aloof
In a world of bursting mortar!
Let the school-children fumble their sums
In a half-dead language;
Let the censor be busy on the books; pull down the
    Georgian slums;

Let the games be played in Gaelic.
Let them grow beet-sugar; let them build
A factory in every hamlet;
Let them pigeon-hole the souls of the killed
Into sheep and goats, patriots and traitors.
And the North, where I was a boy,
Is still the North, veneered with the grime of Glasgow,
Thousands of men whom nobody will employ
Standing at the corners, coughing.

Awareness of the transience of life became, not unnaturally, a deep feeling of anxiety in his war-time poems, but later his dark dislike of much of contemporary life was replaced by a renewed delight in words, momentary joys offsetting his consciousness of death. His posthumous *The Burning Perch* (1963) shows a return to the classical sensibility which had so effectively contributed to his 1936 translation of the *Agamemnon* of Aeschylus and shaped such admirable radio plays as his *Christopher Columbus* and *The Dark Tower*.

MacNeice's saturnine talents and left-wing views were matched by those of his contemporary **John Hewitt** (1907-1987), whose exploration of poetry in Ulster marked his return to his roots. Believing his socialism was hindering his career in the Belfast Museum and Art Gallery (where he worked from 1930 to 1957), he moved to become Director of the Herbert Arts Gallery and Museum in Coventry. Much of his political outlook, his urban socialism, was shaped by English radicalism, though he felt himself merely a guest in England. But when he returned to Belfast in 1972, he wrote sharply intelligent poems emphasising his sense of belonging to the Ulster community, insisting upon his particular kind of Irish nationality, that of the planter stock, 'once alien here' but now as native as anyone else born in Ireland. 'The Glens' puts this clearly:

... Not these my people, of a vainer faith
and a more violent lineage. My dead
lie in the steepled hillock of Kilmore
in a fat country rich with bloom and fruit.
My days, to busy days I owe the world,
are bound to paved unerring roads and rooms
heavy with talk of politics and art.
I cannot spare more than a common phrase
of crops and weather when I pace these lanes
and pause at hedge gap spying on their skill,
so many fences stretch between our minds.
I fear their creed as we have always feared
the lifted hand between the mind and truth.
I know their savage history of wrong
and would at moments lend an eager voice,
if voice avail, to set that tally straight.

And yet no other corner in this land
offers in shape and colour all I need
for sight to torch the mind with living light.

Hewitt exhibits a tough strength in the honesty and technical skill of his poetry which is coming to be increasingly appreciated.

W R Rodgers (1909-69) was a Presbyterian minister in Co Armagh, before going to the BBC in 1945. There he was responsible for many broadcasts on Irish life and literature; *Irish Literary Portraits* (1972) conveys the flavour of good talk about writers and their work. His own poetry is remembered for *Europa and The Bull* (1952), where the pulls of romanticism and puritanism create a lively imaginative and sensuous world, drawing upon his pagan and Christian interests; 'The Net' illustrates something of this tension:

Quick, woman in your net
Catch the silver I fling!

O I am deep in your debt,
Draw tight, skin-tight, the string,
And rake the silver in.
No fisher ever yet
Drew such a cunning ring.
[...]
But I, being man, can kiss
And bed-spread-eagle too;
All flesh shall come to this,
Being less than angel is,
Yet higher far in bliss
As it entwines with you.
Come, make no sound, my sweet;
Turn down the candid lamp
And draw the equal quilt
Over our naked guilt.

10. SAMUEL BECKETT AND MODERN DRAMA

A major figure in modern literature, **Samuel Beckett** (1906-1989) did not write a great deal: two volumes of verse, a collection of short stories, five novels (three originally written in French), some short plays and shorter pieces; but this output has earned him literary immortality as well as the Nobel Prize for Literature. Beckett taught briefly in Belfast, Paris and Dublin; he then spent five somewhat unsettled years before settling in Paris in 1937. There he met Joyce, on whose *Finnegans Wake* he published his first article in 1929. After a critical study of Proust (1931) he wrote an unsuccessful novel, *Dream of Fair to Middling Women* (1992) and then completed *Murphy* (1938).

In this burlesque novel Murphy, an Irishman in London, is the mouthpiece for some of Beckett's philosophical concepts. He is split Cartesianly, between body and mind; he pursues nationalism; he wants to reach nothingness.

Beckett mocks some Irish subjects, disliking nationalism and the clichés of the literary revival. Murphy works in a lunatic asylum, ties himself into a rocking chair, withdrawing into his own mind and dying in a fire caused by a faulty gas pipe.

Beckett received the Croix de Guerre for his work for the French Resistance in the war, during which he wrote *Watt* (1953), another philosophic novel, in which the protagonist works as a servant in a big house, ascending the domestic hierarchy until he reaches the bedroom of the owner, Mr Knott; he is then thrown out. Watt wants to see order in the universe. He has tried to make sense of Mr Knott; he is a logical positivist who cannot make sense of nothing. Human life is seen to be illogical and yet it exists. The novel abounds not only in anecdotes but lists.

After *Watt* Beckett wrote his next three novels in French: *Molloy* (1951; Beckett's English version 1955); *Malone Meurt* (1957; Beckett's English version *Malone Dies*, 1956); and *L'Innommable* (1953; *The Unnameable*, 1959). *Molloy* is a desolate novel of despair and death, life being an exile for nothingness; but death is no answer. In *Malone Dies* desperation is offset by black humour. Malone's memories allow him to ponder the reason for suffering; he is waiting for death, in effect for nothing. The Unnameable in the third novel of the trilogy laments the time wasted in the narration of Murphy, Molloy and Malone: he is not certain of anything. The novel ends with a contradictory situation – a wish to go on talking, balanced by a fierce dislike of language.

Comment C'Est (1961; *How It Is*, 1964) reduces words to a minimum. Beckett has reversed Joyce's exuberant linguistic experimentation, for here words are few indeed: the 'I' of the novel crawling through muck – a disembodied voice employing energetic brief bursts of speech – cannot communicate because only his voice is present. Pim, his target, has forgotten how to talk and is tortured but vanishes, leaving only the voice of 'I'.

This minimalism conveys doubts about human existence and the nature of the self. The fragmented narratives are concerned with the division between mind and the 'reality'. Beckett's most famous handling of these ideas, which made him famous internationally as an innovator, occurred in 1953 when his play *En Attendant Godot* (1952; English version *Waiting for Godot*, 1954) was produced, to challenge audiences from then on. Who is Godot for whom the tramps Vladimir and Estragon are waiting? Their conversation contains parody; the play appears to be about man in time and how he copes with this.

How the play's audiences cope with the problems raised by this play and its successors seemed to Beckett to explain its success; they have sought to give it symbolical or allegorical meaning but Beckett has remarked that the key word in his plays is 'perhaps'. His drama is inconclusive then, but witty and inventive in its grotesque incidents but surprisingly the stoical elements can sometimes outbalance the grotesque or macabre. In *Fin de Partie* (1957; English version *Endgame*, 1958), for instance, only Clov the servant can walk, though he cannot sit down. Hamm, blind and paralysed, who bullies him, cannot walk, nor can his parents who have lost their legs in an accident and are in ash-bins. (Perhaps they derive from Yeats's idea, put in 'Samhain: 1902', of rehearsing actors in barrels so that they could forget gesture and 'have their minds free to think of speech for a while'.) They joke together before Nell dies. Beckett portrays a situation where nothing is known or is likely to be.

His subsequent plays used words even less. In *Acte Sans Paroles* (1957; English version *Act Without Words*, 1958) the possibilities of mime are explored. Later he develops Yeats's exploration of dance in *Quad*, using wordlessness to good effect in television plays such as *Ghost Trio*, while images of mortality recur in *A Piece of Monologue* with its funeral motif:

> Grey light. Rain pelting. Umbrellas round a grave. Seen from above. Streaming black canopies.

In *Happy Days* (1961) there are were two characters, one buried to the waist in the first act, to the neck in the second, while her husband is hardly seen. *Krapp's Last Tape* (1958) was a monologue in which the title character, aged sixty-nine, listens to and comments savagely on a tape recording he had made thirty years before in a vain attempt to recapture the intensity of his youth. The minimalism continued. *Come and Go* (1965) is economic with words, there being but 121 of them. *Breath* (1969) is even more so, lasting only thirty seconds. *Not I* (1973), another monologue, is spoken by an actor whose 'mouth' only is illuminated.

BRENDAN BEHAN

The image of a wild, drunken, outrageous Irishman sometimes clouds consideration of **Brendan Behan** (1923-1964) as a writer. His autobiography *Borstal Boy* (1958) comes out of his somewhat turbulent youth. From a republican family, he was arrested for his part in an IRA bombing campaign in Liverpool in 1939, and spent three years in a Borstal institution. He subsequently tried to kill a detective and served five years of a fourteen-year sentence at the Curragh. *The Quare Fellow* proved a success in Dublin and London but *The Hostage* (1958; first produced in an Irish version, *An Giall*, that year) is a better piece of theatre. It is set in a brothel and the action revolves round an English soldier seized, brought to Dublin from Northern Ireland as a hostage (an IRA man is to be executed in Belfast); he falls in love with an Irish girl who is a servant. The brothel is managed by a former IRA man and owned by an eccentric English aristocrat who speaks Gaelic. The play mocks the author as well as political absolutism:

> [...] The author should have sung that one.
>
> PAT: That's if the thing has an author.
>
> SOLDIER: Brendan Behan, he's too anti-British.
>
> OFFICER: Too anti-Irish, you mean. Bejasus, wait till we get him back home. We'll give him what-for for making fun of the Movement.
>
> SOLDIER [to audience]: He doesn't mind coming over here and taking your money.
>
> PAT: He'd sell his country for a pint.

Behan's health suffered from drink and diabetes and he then wrote scrappy books built upon anecdotes and gossipy memories: *Brendan Behan's Island* (1962) and *Brendan Behan's New York* (1964).

HUGH LEONARD and JOHN B KEANE

Hugh Leonard (John Keyes Byrne, b 1926) was an Irish civil servant until 1959 when he moved to Manchester to work for Granada Television, two of his plays *The Big Birthday* (staged in 1956) and *Madigan's Lock* (1958) having been produced in the Abbey. *Stephen D* (an adaptation of Joyce's *Stephen Hero* and *A Portrait of the Artist as a Young Man*, first produced in 1962) and *A Walk on the Water* (1960; published in *Selected Plays* 1992) having proved successful, he returned to Dublin. While continuing to exercise his skill in writing and adapting material for television he has written some entertaining stage plays set in Ireland, his autobiographical *Da* the best of them. Two amusing and unsentimental prose autobiographical studies are *Home Before Night* (1979) and *Out After Dark* (1989).

Another very popular dramatist is **John B Keane** (b 1928), born in Listowel, Co Kerry, a publican who wrote his first play *Give* in 1959. A series of popular successes has followed, the best of them probably *The Field* (1965) and *Big Maggie* (1969), a blend of realism and melodrama. His fictional letters (from a TD, a priest, a farmer, a publican, a civic guard and others) have also been very popular, as well as his novels *The Bodhran Makers* (1986) and *Durango* (1992).

BRIAN FRIEL

There is no question about **Brian Friel**'s (b 1929) dominance as a dramatist since *The Enemy Within* was produced in 1962. His next play *Philadelphia, Here I Come* (1964) gained him international repute. It centres upon a young man, Gar O'Donnell, during the night before he emigrates to America: his two selves Private Gar and Public Gar are played by two actors. The play punctures bravado, reveals the stagnation of village life and criticises the materialism that offers an easier, but emptier, life in America. Friel followed this with various plays exploring love, notably *The Loves of Cass Maguire* (1966). He turned to political subjects in *The Mundy Scheme* (1969) and *The Gentle Island* (1971). Next came four related plays – *The Freedom of the City* (1973) was stimulated by events in Northern Ireland; *Volunteers* (1975) went back to Irish history. *Aristocrats* (1979) analysed the situation of a big house family, also in elegaic terms: a death not a wedding is the ironic focus of the family reunion. The son of the house mythologises the life of its owners, for whom there is no place in 20th century Ireland: the house with all its oppressive atmosphere will have to be sold. In *Living Quarters* (1977) Friel wrote with Euripides' *Hippolytus* in mind; he is Chekhovian, however, in his analysis of a middle-class well-to-do Catholic family. The jesting chat of the family reveals the tragic matter of the play. Friel is experimenting with an idea here, that the characters know their own destiny, a result he achieves by having a commentator, Sir, on stage throughout the play. More experimentation followed in the four monologues of *Faith Healer* (1979).

Then Friel, a schoolmaster until 1960, after that a full-time writer, became founder-director of the Field Day Theatre Company in 1980. One result was his brilliant play *Translations* (1980), which deals with the mapping of Ireland in the 1830s by the Ordnance Survey. The play is set in a hedge school in a small town in Donegal into which there comes a detachment of Royal Engineers who have surveyed the locality and are now attempting to anglicise local names for the maps. More than local reactions are involved, however, for this is also a discussion of the cultural detriment that comes with the loss of a language and the effect of a colonial power upon indigenous culture. The play carries a view put forward by several writers in the 1970s and 1980s that by not knowing Irish they had been deprived of a heritage.

Afraid that Ireland will become 'a shabby imitation of a third-rate American state', Friel is deeply concerned with the defining role of language:

> We are more concerned with defining our Irishness than with pursuing it. We want to know what the word native means, what the word foreign means. We want to know

have the words any meaning at all. And persistent considerations like these erode old certainties and help clear the building site.

There were several reasons for the decline of Irish as a mother-tongue. In 1600 the majority of the people in Ireland spoke it; by 1900 fewer than five percent. Among the causes were economic pressure, the effect of the National Schools system set up in 1831 in which the sole medium of instruction was English, the effect of the Famines of the 1840s in reducing the population by death or emigration. *Translations* deals with language, with the struggle between the Irish and the English; it makes the point that there was a clash between two cultures. It shows the impossibility of translating place names appropriately and the apparent tragedy of the love affair between the English officer and the local girl Máire (who seem to be triumphing over the problems in communication caused by the different languages of the lovers) suggests a pessimistic view of the basic problem between the English and the Irish.

In *Making History* (1988) Friel examines happenings before and after the crucial Battle of Kinsale (1601). Hugh O'Neill, the Earl of Tyrone, through his reluctant decision to fight the English, in effect destroyed the old Irish civilisation. Then, sharing in the 'Flight of the Earls' from Ireland, he disintegrated in drunken exile in Rome. Friel is concerned with the mythology. His O'Neill would like the truth told, not the myth created by Archbishop Lombard, a Counter-Reformation myth of Catholic Irish patriotism becoming nationalism. Friel questions language in the play, revealing the different cultural values which different languages convey; this play weaves them together in what he calls a dramatic fiction, using some real and some imagined events in Hugh O'Neill's life, realising that an historical text is a kind of literary artefact.

Dancing at Lughnasa (1990) departs from Friel's apparent previous preoccupation with history and language: art is to fill a vacuum since politics are corrupt or barren. The play uses time skilfully. Its action set in Lughnasa, a place which seems ahistorical, at once primal in its harbouring of fierce forces, but also present in an autobiographical sense. The story is slight, but there is no resentment at the failure of drama or words to present reality. Instead music and dance give fluidity, while memory and forgetfulness combine to suspend the play out of some larger actions. It centres upon the characters' experiences: history happens outside the lives of the five unmarried sisters and Uncle Jack, the mentally-disturbed missionary priest, and Micheal, the illegitimate son of Chris who acts as narrator. The flow of a continuous present tense relies upon memory – that is personal truth made real. In a particular memory, Micheal remarks that 'atmosphere is more real than incident and everything is simultaneously actual and illusory'.

THOMAS KILROY and THOMAS MURPHY

Thomas Kilroy (b 1934), educated at University College, Dublin, taught at various universities before becoming Professor of English at University College, Galway, from 1978 to 1989. He has gained most reputation as a playwright through *Talbot's Box* (1979) set in working-class Dublin, in which Matt Talbot struggles to keep his own vision of God intact: another 'irreducible division' between personal visions and the claims of society upon its individual members. *Tea and Sex and Shakespeare* (1976) is a clever comedy about an anti-hero author. Kilroy has adapted various plays by Chekhov and Ibsen. His novel *The Big Chapel* (1971) is a powerful, gripping novel about 19th century

Catholicism, a tense struggle set in Co Kilkenny between local practice and the ultramontane theories of the time.

Born in Tuam, Co Galway, **Tom Murphy** (b 1935) taught metalwork, emigrating to England to become a full-time writer in 1961. His one act play *On the Outside* (1959) and its matching *On the Inside* (1979) use a dance-hall as a symbol, respectively, of exclusion from the excitement and inclusion in its tensions. *A Whistle in the Dark*, rejected by the Abbey, has echoes of Synge in its fratricide, its characters lost in their violent feuding.

In *A Crucial Week in the Life of a Grocer's Assistant* (1969) Murphy continued to explore contradictions between the excitement (and the enticement) of emigration and what is, ultimately, peasant realism as presented by so many Abbey dramatists. After his return to Ireland in 1970, he wrote *Morning after Optimism* (1971), a play in which idealism is set against the reality through a variety of theatrical techniques. His next play, *The Sanctuary Lamp* (1975), attacked for its anticlericalism, continued Murphy's exploration of the tensions between the idealism which underlay the creation of the Irish Free State, allied to the prescriptiveness of the Catholic church, and the reality of life in Ireland. These tensions erupt in violence and the Ireland that the plays portray is one where men's anger is occasionally balanced by the resilience of women, something evident in *Conversations on a Homecoming* (1985) where Michael's return from America is celebrated by his friends. *Bailegangaire* (1985) and *Too Late for Logic* (1989), a comedy, are more sanguine.

STEWART PARKER and FRANK MCGUINNESS

Stewart Parker (1941-1988), educated at Queen's University, Belfast, was a dramatist who combined an ability to capture audiences with an originality of approach and a basic faith in individual capacity for fundamental decency. His historic plays were *Northern Star* (1984), *Heavenly Bodies* (1986) and *Pentecost* (1987) which deals with the Ulster Workers' strike of 1974 with fine dramatic skill. His radio play *The Kamikazi Ground Staff Reunion Dinner* (1980) is unforgettable.

Frank McGuinness (b 1953) born in Buncrana, Co Donegal, and educated at Univeristy College, Dublin, has written poems – his first collection was *Booterstown* (1994) – and short stories but is mainly known for his plays. *Factory Girls* (1982) shows the influence of Brian Friel; it was followed by several plays, of which *Observe the Sons of Ulster Marching towards the Somme* (1985) has been particularly successful. His *Carthaginians, The Gatherers* and *Innocence* all share a sharpness of vision and are professionally well-shaped plays. Various translations and adaptations by McGuinness have been staged and his BBC television plays have also added to his reputation as a playwright.

11. NOVELISTS FROM THE 1950s ON

IRIS MURDOCH

Three very different novelists began publishing in the 1950s. **Iris Murdoch** (b 1919), an Oxford philosophy don born in Dublin and brought up in London, has brought to her fiction philosophical theory and an awareness of the power of passion. Some of her novels are extremely funny. Nearly all run to complex plots and she is very representative of her time in her exploration of how individuals react to large issues. Her first novel *Under the Net* (1954) remains her most picaresque and rattles on at high speed most entertainingly. Permissiveness permeates subsequent novels about personal choices: *The Flight from the Enchanter* (1956), *The Sandcastle* (1957), *The Bull* (1958), *A Severed Head* (1961) and *An Unofficial Rose* (1962).

The Unicorn (1963) and *The Red and the Green* (1965) are set in Ireland. These are not her most effective novels: the former is very melodramatic, the latter an investigation into divided loyalties at the time of the 1916 Rising. She is more at ease when her milieu is modish, bohemian London in the permissive 1960s. There is an artificiality in the novels written up to *Bruno's Dream* (1969), the plots becoming more complex, the actions and talk exaggerated, over-clever in fact. With *The Nice and the Good* (1968) and *A Fairly Honourable Defeat* (1970) there is, however, a strengthening of the style, maintained as far as *The Sea, The Sea* (1978) but somewhat slackened in subsequent novels. Iris Murdoch's writing on philosophical topics includes *Sartre* (1953).

BRIAN MOORE

In his early novels **Brian Moore** (b 1919) brought an impressive gift for narration and the portrayal of individual characters to bear upon the restrictive life imposed by religious rigidity. In *Judith Hearne* (1955), *The Lonely Passion of Judith Hearne* (1956) and *The Feast of Lupercal* (1957) he explores the social aridity ensuing from conflict between sexual impulses and spiritual con-straints. Judith Hearne, a spinster, fails to conform and eventually experiences stresses and lonely sadness which end in her senility. *The Emperor of Ice-Cream* (1965), however, concentrates upon a young Catholic teenager's troubled relationship with his bigoted father, the German bombing of Belfast liberating the boy into maturity.

A later novel, *The Doctor's Wife* (1976), the tale of a mature married woman's adventuring into a love affair with a younger man, again emphasises the limitations and social pressures of a conformist society. The woman's husband, a Belfast doctor, is portrayed as a highly respectable figure in the community, who emerges as a limited, insensitive, out-raged philistine when he realises the actuality of his wife's infidelity.

After migrating to Canada in 1948 Moore explored fresh material. *The Luck of Ginger Coffey* (1960) develops a greater ability to handle life as comic, the protagonist, an Irish immigrant, eventually overcoming various failures to cope with the very different kind of social situations he meets in Canada. The difference between North American society and Northern Irish is further developed in *An Answer from Limbo* (1962), another story of how differently Belfast emigrants react to New York's streamlined way of living. North American life allows Mary Dunne in *I am Mary Dunne* (1968), in feminist fashion, to search for her own space, to search, somewhat irresponsibly, for who and what she really is. *Fergus* (1970), not generally taken to be written at Moore's highest level, is, nonetheless, well worth reading. Imagined conversations with the dead promote powerful evocations of guilt as Fergus contemplates how he has changed, from responding to the mores of his father's society to becoming part of the rootlessness of North American life.

The Great Victorian Collection (1975) continues to exploit the use of dream or hallucination to explore reality. While *The Revolution Spirit* (1971) is firmly based upon the kidnapping and death of a Quebec politician, *Catholics*

(1972) is another of Moore's concerned contemplations of Catholicism. In this case, when the Catholic church's close tyranny is contrasted with that of the fluid anonymity of North America, the resultant loss of accepted ideals and the supportive stability provided by ritual and established order creates a vacuum to be feared. *The Mangan Inheritance* (1979) returns us to Ireland, the predominant theme being a contrast between what could come of freedom and the restrained behaviour imposed by inherited values: it is a chilling book.

Moore has continued to explore the relationship between religious belief and authority. Apart from a novel about 17th century Canada, *Black Robe* (1985), he has dealt with contemporary situations. *Cold Heaven* (1983), set in Ulster, shows us the complex moral situation of a man whose wife is a hostage while he drives a bomb to a human target. *The Colour of Blood* (1987) is less convincing in its portrayal of an individual's problems in a communist state, but *No Other Life* (1993), placed in Haiti with all the murderous violence there, concentrates upon the pressure of political imperatives upon human life.

Within Moore's variety of subject matter we are never far from his basic intellectual preoccupations with the impact of religion and politics upon individuals. His novels tend to contain explicit descriptions of sex and, more economically treated, explosive violence. He can certainly be relied upon to hold his readers' attention and leave them with serious issues to contemplate.

AIDAN HIGGINS

Aidan Higgins (b 1927) is best known for *Langrishe, Go Down* (1966), a story of the decay of yet another big house family. It followed a volume of short stories, *Felo de Se* (1960; entitled *Asylum and Other Stories*, it was republished in 1971) several of which reflect the author's experience of travelling and working in South Africa. An autobiographical account of his life there appeared in *Images of Africa* (1971; entitled *Ronda Gorge and Other Precipices*, it was republished in 1989).

A novel, *Lions of the Grunewald* (1993), also draws upon his travels for background settings. But his *Donkey's Years, Scenes from a Receding Past* (1977) is an eminently readable reconstruction of his Catholic family's decline from landowning in Co Kildare to a succession of dwellings in the neighbourhood of Dublin. The author's relatively affluent childhood is balanced by subsequent sadness, equally well drawn, conveying casualness impressionistically yet with convincing clarity.

WILLIAM TREVOR

William Trevor (b 1928, pseudonym of **William Cox**) can cast a compassionate eye over human foibles and write of them with a detached, urbane irony. He has been intrigued by the variety of human behaviour and he has added a variety of human beings to the stock of fiction. Whether he chooses the short story or the novel he paces his narrative precisely and persuasively. He may have learned his architectonic skills before beginning to write at the age of thirty. By then he had taught in several schools and created a highly successful career as a sculptor and wood-carver, but abandoned it in 1960 because he couldn't 'get the people in my head into the sculpture'. He had to write short stories, he said, to bring them to life.

His first novel, *A Standard of Behaviour*, was published in 1958. He maintained himself by working as a copywriter in an advertising agency until 1964. That year his second novel, *The Old Boys* (1964), which contains one of his nastier characters, Basil Jaraby, a child molester, won the Hawthornden Prize. *The Day We Got Drunk on Cake and Other Stories* (1967) was his first collection of short stories. The title story of *The Ballroom of Romance* (1972) has proved very popular, and is probably the best of many versions of his work to be filmed or televised: it has been well-described as a poignant evocation of a rural Ireland where men drink and women wait.

As Trevor wrote in his *Collected Stories* (1972), he considers the short story 'a very very difficult form. Novels can be ragbags and go wandering off but a good short story must leave a smear or dab of paint on the mind from which the reader has to do the rest of the work'. His own novels are certainly not ragbags and do not go wandering off; he creates settings for his characters economically but very effectively, as in *Mrs Eckdorf at O'Neill's Hotel* (1969) and *Fools of Fortune* (1983) 'gravely written and often hilarious'. *Reading Turgenev,* the first of two novels in *Two Lives* (1991) is equally moving, equally masterly in its narration.

Trevor is just as at home in English or Irish settings: for instance, his *The Children of Dynmouth* (1976) has its teenager, Timothy Gedge, terrifying an English holiday town by the sea, and *Lovers of Their Time* (1978) has its middle-aged romantic episode set in a Paddington hotel. Stories such as 'Attracta' (1978) and 'Beyond the Pale' return us through a compassionate narrative to sterner stuff, for Irish subjects have largely occupied Trevor since the 1980s.

Residence in Devon has given him the distance he requires, for from it he can conjure up the essence of his Irish novels and their increasing use of violent episodes. *Fools of Fortune* (1983) was followed by *The Silence in the*

Garden (1988), in which Trevor uses the familiar theme of the big house, here the setting for the dying twilight, the death of the Ascendancy. A cousin of the owners of Carriglas, Sarah Pollexfen, comes to the house as a governess and becomes deeply involved in its secrets, finally dying in it. Here we also have the IRA, murder in error, all the confusion encapsulated, the human chaos engendered by a tyrannic past, sometimes true, sometimes magical.

Trevor is at his best here and the reasons for his having won so many awards – those of the Royal Society of Literature, the Allied Irish Banks Prize, the Whitbread Prize – are obvious. He writes not only with sympathy but discernment about the wide range of characters he creates, Catholic and Protestant, sensible and silly, young and old.

In *The Silence in the Garden* he gives us a devastating analysis of social minutiae; a vignette shows how Mrs Moledy (who keeps a boarding house and with whom John James, son of the big house, is having an affair, almost against his will) behaves at a wedding in Carriglas:

> Noticing that her glass had become empty, Mrs Moledy rose and made her way into the house through the open French windows. 'There's nothing can't be put right with a drop of Paddy,' was a favourite axiom of the big trawler-man who came into Myley Flynn's, a fresh-faced man with exploded veins all over his nose and cheeks. In her own view Power's was the better drink, but what wasn't there you couldn't have. She found the bottle of Paddy among the sherry decanters on the sideboard.
>
> Afterwards Mrs Moledy recalled making several journeys to the sideboard. She recalled saying to herself how partylike the flowers were, and how the long table looked lovely with its clean white tablecloths. Three old sheepdogs came and slumped down beside her, as tame and friendly as you could ask for. 'Isn't it nice here?' she said

whenever the young one appeared with something else for the table, but the only response she received was a giggle.

In time other people appeared. His brother peered out of the dining-room, dressed up in fancy togs. A female with forget-me-nots on her dress came out and spoke to her. She thought it was the sister so she held out her hand, even though she was puzzled by the reduced size of her and wondered if she'd suffered an attack of something.

'I'm Noreen Moledy,' she said. 'We never met.'

While he is passionately interested in places, as is shown by his *A Writer's Ireland* (1984), a delightful book and a superb study of Irish landscape in literature, Trevor portrays people with infinite skill. They are often eccentric, bizarre even, but always realistic. Their conversation caught completely convincingly, their natures understood, their tales told with an outstanding mastery of the art of fiction.

JENNIFER JOHNSTON

Jennifer Johnston (b 1930) is skilled in building up and maintaining atmosphere. Her narration carries readers along with its sense of time, at an apparently leisurely pace at first, then hurls them into explosive endings as private worlds of love or understanding come up against old prejudices, old divisions, old violence renewed. Born in Dublin and educated at Trinity College, Dublin, the daughter of the playwright Denis Johnston and the actress Shelagh Richards, she examines the uncertain role of the Anglo-Irish in the new independent Ireland in such novels as *The Captains and the Kings* (1972) and *The Gates* (1973), a particularly sensitive study of misunderstanding. In this novel the position of the Anglo-Irish is examined with some deft symbolism:

Just off the road leading to the Major's house, the Protestant church crouched like a little old lady, embarrassed at
being found some place she had no right to be, behind a
row of yew trees. The other end of the village, on a slight
eminence, a semi-cathedral, topped by an ornate gold
cross, preened itself triumphantly.

The Old Jest (1979) centres on a young and innocent Protestant girl who helps a gunman on the run. His death has a
laconic, convincing inevitability:

She walked through the soldiers, then she stopped and
looked back. He had thrown his bag on to the sand and
was fumbling in his pocket for the gun. He took it out and
looked at it for a moment, and then threw it down beside
the bag. Then they shot him. Two, Three shots. Running.

Social extremes can meet in friendship, in *How Many Miles
to Babylon?* (1974), in religion in *Shadows on Our Skin*
(1977) and *The Invisible Worm* (1991), again returning to
the big house theme. *The Railway Station Man* (1984)
develops the idea of *The Old Jest* further; its individual
lovers are doomed by outside force. These are no saccha-
rine novels. Their tragedies convince: they have a limpidity
of style, a naturalness of dialogue, and a sure handling of
plot. All these add up to an impressive achievement.

EDNA O'BRIEN and JULIA O'FAOLAIN

Within three years **Edna O'Brien** (b 1930) had her three
first novels published; they were *The Country Girls* (1960);
The Lonely Girl (1962; it was republished as *The Girl with
Green Eyes* in 1964); and *Girls in Their Married Bliss* (1963).
Written in a naive, somewhat breathlessly intense style
these portray innocent, indeed vulnerable, girls growing up
in the puritan Ireland of the 1940s and 1950s. Later novels
have been written in an equally highly charged but tidier

style; they include *August is a Wicked Month* (1964), *A Pagan Place* (1971), *Night* (1972) and *The High Road* (1988). *House of Splendid Isolation* (1994) is fashionably concerned with the IRA, in this case a gunman's relationship with the woman whose house he has taken over. Short stories also consider Edna O'Brien's favourite subjects, love and sexual relationships; they have been selected in *Fanatic Heart* (1982).

Julia O'Faolain (b 1932), educated at University College, Dublin, the University of Rome and the Sorbonne, is a skilled translator as well as an impressive writer of fiction. Her first collection of short stories, *We Might See Sights* (1968), demonstrated her sharp wit. She is economical but highly effective in descriptions of characters:

> Rosie had blonde, naturally curly hair, abundant as an aureole and alive with lice. She had a mouthful of bossy teeth and a foamy laugh.

Her first novel, *Godded and Codded* (1970), showed she could maintain this punchiness at greater length. *Women in the Wall* (1975) is an historical novel full of telling detail set in the brutal world of 6th century Gaul where a group of nuns search for spiritual peace. Very different is *No Country for Young Men* (1980) satirical in its theme, the brutality of ruthless, dogmatic, political mythology, yet sympathetic to the human suffering engendered by the inevitable insensitivity of such a society.

The Obedient Wife (1982) convincingly portrays Carla, a wife torn between the demands of a husband absent in Italy and a lover present in Los Angeles, the former urging her to sexual freedom, the latter a priest who wants to marry her. This is all deftly done, the humdrum detail underpinning the dialogue and the basic dilemma, the strange pull between loyalty to a universal church and a small family; it is full of sharp observation:

> Sybil in her car looked like the old woman who lived in a shoe. The car itself could have been a fertility emblem. It was big, rabbit-brown and always cluttered with a spill of Kleenex boxes, book bags, children's possessions and children themselves.

The Irish Signorina (1984) was followed by *The Judas Cloth* (1992), a study of the clerical politics behind the career of Pius IX who moved from reform to reactionary conservatism. Julia O'Faolain's searching novels continue to question orthodoxies and to enlarge the cosmopolitan range of her subject matter.

JOHN MCGAHERN

After being educated at St. Patrick's College, Drumcondra, and University College, Dublin, **John McGahern** (b 1934) took up a teaching position in St John the Baptist's National School in Dublin. While teaching he wrote *The Barracks* (1961), which successfully conveys a stifling atmosphere, the heroine dying of cancer and living in a state of doubt. His next novel, *The Dark* (1965) was banned and McGahern dismissed from his school without explanation, the clerical managers of the school refusing to reinstate him. In this novel McGahern addresses his hero directly, a technique which distances the author from his subject very effectively:

> You were walking through the rain of Galway with your father and you could laugh purely, without bitterness, for the first time, and it was a kind of happiness, at its heart the terror of an unclear recognition of the reality that set you free, touching you with as much foreboding as the sodden leaves falling in this day or any cliché.

McGahern moved to London and then lived in Spain and the United States before returning to Ireland to live in Co

Leitrim. *The Leavetaking* (1974; revised heavily in 1984) was followed by *The Pornographer* (1979) which sees the sexual freedom of the liberated 1960s packaged as pornography and the apparent liberation as completely false.

Amongst Women (1990) is an impressive novel, set in the West Midlands, the region in which McGahern grew up, to which he has returned and which he understands well. Its repressive society is captured with realism and the characters are psychologically convincing. It is the story of an ageing farmer, a former republican and present domestic tyrant, who is loved by the exasperated women whom he bullies and is baffled when they do not obey his dictates. McGahern's study is a latterday echo of Brinsley MacNamara's fiction, but so concentrated with remorseless realism on a small number of people forced into conflict with the formal pressures of conformity that it possesses lasting literary value.

MAEVE BINCHY and BERNARD McLAVERTY

Maeve Binchy (b 1940), born in Dublin and educated at University College, Dublin, moved from teaching to journalism. Her first stories, about London life, were collected in *Central Line* (1971) and *Victoria Line* (1980); then followed *Dublin 4* (1982) and *The Lilac Bus* (1984). She then began to write novels which have proved extremely popular: they include *Light a Penny Candle* (1982), *Echoes* (1985), *Firefly Summer* (1987), perhaps the best of them, *Silver Wedding* (1988) and *Circle of Friends* (1990). The reason for the appeal of her fiction is that her novels exude a comfortable kind of certainty: a sense of the family within a community, which is very cleverly achieved though often at the cost of overmuch sentimentality in their cosy conclusions.

Bernard McLaverty (b 1942) has written several collections of stories, the best-known *The Great Profundo* (1987), while his novels *Lamb* (1980), a study of the relationship between a staff member of a Borstal institution and a young pupil, and *Cal* (1983), an account of a terrorist's love affair with the widow of the man he killed, have giving him continuing acclaim, added to by his recent volume of stories, *Walking the Dog* (1994).

JOHN BANVILLE

John Banville (b 1945), the present literary editor of the *Irish Times*, was born in Wexford. He worked for a time with Aer Lingus and then on the *Irish Press*. Very much a modern intellectual, very much a modern novelist able to enjoy freedom in technique and subject matter, he explores the relationship between creative imagination and apparent reality. He has enjoyed using the traditional motif of the big house, sometimes self-consciously, sometimes easily, as a structure for some of his fiction.

Long Larkin (1976), a collection of short stories, and *Nightspawn* (1971), a thriller, preceded *Birchwood* (1973), set in the Irish countryside, which is a welcome addition to the general stock of big house novels. Banville's originality of mind declares itself in a quartet of novels in which he makes an imaginative approach to the likely thoughts of distinguished scientists: *Copernicus* (1976, which won the James Tait Black Prize), *Kepler* (1981; won the *Guardian* fiction prize), *The Newton Letter* (1982) and *Mefisto* (1986). An intellectual cosmopolitanism informs these novels. Banville has given a philosophical cast to his fiction through what is at times a deliberately allusive style, which is nonetheless anchored in commonsense, as his descriptions tend to be rooted in the Wexford scenery in which he grew up.

In *The Book of Evidence* (1989), which won the Guinness Peat Aviation Award, he returns to Ireland, the subject a murder reminiscent of one that set respectable Dublin by the ears some years ago. This novel is most impressive; its flowing prose with all its knowing irony, its blend of lyricism and a sense of loss, and its confession which is so cleverly constructed, make this book not only compelling but most disturbing. The central character, Frederick Charles St John Vanderweld Montgomery reveals his thoughts and his moods in a way that startles while it convinces, particularly in the account of his arrest; the account of the murder itself is challengingly horrific. *The Ghosts* (1993) is a worthy sequel, itself followed by *Athena* (1995), an exploration of love. In his fiction Banville has generally reacted very effectively indeed against what he considers the obsessions of Irish fiction: politics, religion and repressed sexuality.

RODDY DOYLE and DERMOT BOLGER

Roddy Doyle (b 1958), born in Dublin, educated at University College, Dublin, worked as a teacher from 1979 to 1993. His novels take over where O'Casey's plays stopped in their use of Dublin speech, lively, imaginative, self-aware; the difference is in the incessant use of expletives and scatology which at times negates the effect of the narrative. *The Commitments* (1989) and *The Snapper* (1990) portray a Dublin working-class family and Doyle's use of Dublin *argot* in them is continued in *The Van* (1991), which conveys the effect of unemployment with a stronger literary mediation of the material.

Paddy Clarke Ha Ha Ha (1993; it won the Booker Prize) is a clever interpretation of a boy's reactions to life about him, his thoughts and speech matching, and the action economically built in. The failure of the parents' marriage is told unsentimentally and, as a result, most effectively. Doyle has written successful plays for stage and television, his dialogue forceful, his capacity to arouse and hold attention the equal of that displayed in his novels.

Somewhat similar in his commitment to contemporary issues is **Dermot Bolger** (b 1959) who founded the Raven Arts Press in 1979. He grew up in Finglas, now a large working-class suburb of Dublin, which provides the scene and much of the material for his novels *Night Shift* (1985) and *The Woman's Daughter* (1987), dealing largely with the plight of abused women, while in *A Second Life* (1994) an adopted child, now grown up, tries to find his mother.

12. CONTEMPORARY POETRY

RICHARD MURPHY

While Austin Clarke was experiencing a poetic rebirth in the 1960s younger poets were establishing themselves with confidence. **Richard Murphy** (b 1927), for instance, moved from his autobiographical volume *Archaeology of Love* (1955) to the distinctive poems of *Sailing to an Island* (1963) which record his experiences and reflections when living on the island of Inishboffin. He rebuilt a Galway hooker, a local sailing vessel, and made a commercial success of using it as transport, hiring it to visitors interested in sailing and fishing.

Two longer poems, 'The Cleggan Disaster' and 'The Woman of the House', a fine elegy for his grandmother, show Murphy to be technically polished; this is particularly pleasing in the sonnets of *The Price of Stone* (1985). While these are intended to keep a portion of the past and memories of his family and friends alive after death, they seem, however, to lack the life of the *Battle of Aughrim* (1968), a narrative poem based on the defeat of the Irish Jacobites in the Williamite war, lamenting it and the continuance of past hatreds into the present. *The Mirror Wall* (1989) links Western concepts with Sri Lankan songs, echoing his own interest in church music and structures.

THOMAS KINSELLA

Thomas Kinsella (b1928), educated at University College, Dublin, was a civil servant before going to Harvard in 1963 where he studied Old Irish, becoming a professor at Temple University, Philadelphia, in 1965, this involving, as in the case of several other Irish academics, holding an American chair and spending about half the year in America, half in Ireland.

His first volume *Poems* (1956) was followed by *Another September* (1958) which explores aspects of love. *Downstream* (1962) contains several trenchant and gloomy poems, and *Nightwalker and Other Poems* (1968) considers the human capacity for destructiveness.

The early influence of Auden was succeeded by that of William Carlos Williams and other American poets, Kinsella making few concessions to readers of his poetry and in his criticism making few concessions to any concept of an Irish culture not set within two rigid traditions. This is somewhat in the spirit of the turn of the century Irish Irelanders and of the later pronouncements of the contemporary critic Seamus Deane. Kinsella's best Irish achievement is his translation of the *Táin Bó Cuailnge* (1969); he has also shared with Seán Ó Tuama the editing of *An Duanaire: Poems of the Dispossessed* (1981). His *New Oxford Book of Irish Verse* (1986) is an admirable anthology.

He has published his own poems under his Peppercanister imprint, many of the sequences gathered in *Blood and*

Family (1988), where Kinsella scrutinises his family history. He likes the past while querying its effect, as in 'Tear' and 'Ancestor' which begins:

> I was going up to say something,
> and stopped. Her profile against the curtains
> was old, and dark like a hunting bird's.
>
> It was the way she perched on the high stool,
> staring into herself, with one fist
> gripping the side of the barrier around her desk
> or her head held by something, from inside.
> And not caring for anything around her
> or anyone there by the shelves.
> I caught a faint smell, musky and queer.

EITHNE STRONG

Five years after Kinsella's first volume was published came *Sons of Living* (1961), the first collection of **Eithne Strong** (b 1923). Born in Limerick and educated at Trinity College, Dublin, she worked in the Irish civil service before her marriage and has been a journalist and teacher. She writes wittily in Irish and English about the role of women, about domestic matters and about some minority issues, her poems crisp and economic in their forceful utterance.

Flesh – the Greatest Sin (1980) and her collection *Spatial Nosing* (1993) contain some of her best poems. She has also written short stories and a novel *The Love Riddle* (1993). A typically terse, witty poem is 'Statement to Offspring' where her final line, because of what has gone before, effectively transcends the current cliche in its 'Just allow me room.'

JOHN MONTAGUE

John Montague (b 1929), two years Richard Murphy's senior, came to poetry with an aim of extending contemporary Irish poetry's preoccupation with local interests into international scope. Whereas Brian Coffey and Denis Devlin tended to be preoccupied with continental writers, Montague was also under the influence of American poets, Robert Duncan, for instance; and he thought Ezra Pound as important a mentor for an Irish poet as Eoghán Ó Rathille. After University College, Dublin, he went to Yale and later taught at Berkeley and in the State Universty of New York.

Montague, despite wanting to be a global-regionalist, has touches of the Irish-American about him. His Ulster Catholic background, however, dominates his major work, *The Rough Field* (1972). This links a sequence of different poems together architectonically in a desire to relate past to present. There is very bitter political anger here, perhaps to be explained by the deprivation expressed in the personal poems in his collection *A Slow Dance* (1975). These poems – 'The Muddy Cup', 'Mother Cat', 'A Flowering Absence', and 'The Locket' concern the mother who left him with his Montague relations while taking her other children to her family home, his father living in exile in Brooklyn, a figure who is behind many of Montague's poems.

In *The Rough Field* other material is juxtaposed to counterpoint the poet's own voice. The theme is continued in *The Dead Kingdom* (1984), while *The Great Cloak* (1978) was occupied with love poems. Montague has made much use of short lines, aiming at the conversational style of many modern American poets; he sees himself as a spokesman for a hidden Ulster and he writes evocatively of Garvaghy in Co Tyrone, always aware of the past in a determinist fashion, of the 'two crazed peoples' of Ulster. His poems about his family can be affectionate, as in 'The Silver Flask'; and a journey with his brother is told with graphic sympathy.

JAMES SIMMONS

James Simmons (b 1933) is mainly known for having founded and edited *The Honest Ulsterman* for its first year in 1969. He has taught in Nigeria and the University of Ulster and now runs the Poet's House at Islandmagee, Co Antrim. A series of volumes began with *Late but in Earnest* (1967), nine others intervening before *Poems 1956-1985*. Influenced by a liking for jazz and the blues, Simmons has a lively sense of rhythm, his rhyming is facile and his verses often founded upon sexuality and selfhood can at times carry off a generally cheerful confessional braggadocio but at the risk of lapsing into vulgarity.

BRENDAN KENNELLY

Brendan Kennelly (b 1936) was more cheerful than Montague in his treatment of historical themes in *My Dark Fathers* (1964) – he had previously shared two volumes with Rudi Holzapfel. A Kerryman, a Professor in Trinity College, Dublin, Kennelly is rooted in his Kerry background, an awed awareness, perhaps, of violence arising from it. But he has developed a very personal kind of poetry in which his thought flows freely: kindness keeps breaking out and an understanding of the differences of individual human beings. His written poetry has all the spontaneity of oral tradition but is searching in its investigations.

Kennelly's first long poem *Cromwell* (1983) is the result of scholarly enquiry into the history of the man, that contradictory figure, at once civilised, a lover of his family, of mathematics and music, yet one whose exploits made his name 'eternally hated in Ireland'. This complexity of character challenges Kennelly, the de-mythologiser, stimulating him into the brutal honesty he brings to bear upon the horrors, themselves brutal enough in all conscience. He explores, determinedly, the differences in outlook between the English mind and the Irish mind. The poem's vision of what might be called the Irish nightmare reminds us that contemporary poets viewing the past are very conscious of the present (as in Murphy's *The Battle of Aughrim* or Montague's *The Rough Field*) and its apparently recurring determinist violence. Kennelly, however, does not see violence as endemic or inevitable but rather as something which can erupt anywhere, at any time.

In *The Book of Judas* (1991), another linked sequence of poems, Kennelly has been more successful, for the sombre discussion is enlivened here by several comic interludes in, for instance, 'Eily Kilbride' who once went into the countryside and:

> Saw a horse with a feeding bag over its head
> And thought it was sniffing glue

'The Dinner' has James Joyce dining with the Holy Family, an episode in which Kennelly's subtly ironic humour demands to be read aloud.

The vast tumbling variety of Kennelly's imagination is let loose in this book: it can be coarse, shocking, blasphemous, as it considers betrayal of all kinds. The preface puts his intention well; he wants to capture:

> ... the relentless, pitiless anecdotalism of Irish life, the air swarming with nutty little sexual parables, the platitudinous bonhomie sustained by venemous undercurrents, the casual ferocious gossip, the local industry of remorse-making and spreading, always remembering that life is being parodied, that this Christian culture itself is a parody of what may have been a passion.

That preface was written not out of the experience of Ballylongford, Co Kerry, but of Baile Átha Cliath, Dublin City, which is the subject of *Poetry My Arse* (1995), a 'labyrinth of comic distortion'. Kennelly has a Goldsmithian capacity for laughing at himself, as in 'Front Square' where the poem's protagonist, the poet Ace de Horner, describes him as a 'cute Kerry hoor', his poetry as 'Bad, black, blasphemous rubbish'. Ace de Horner, accompanied by Janey May and Kanooce, the pitbull terrier, moves through Dublin and its reductive, funny bitterness as Kennelly investigates his poet-persona's sense of integrity and deception in the many poems which make up this everyman's epic, this debunking of poetry: 'Nobody has ever heard of poetry! Does it matter?'

Kennelly has tamped his exuberant imagination down into explosive translations of Euripides's *Antigone* (1986) *Medea* (1988) and *The Trojan Women* (1995). Knowing no Greek, like Yeats before him, he nonetheless, like Yeats with Sophocles, gives Euripides a modern voice, the passion of Medea revivified, the fate of the captured Trojan women an invincible indictment of war's inhumanity. Kennelly is interested in the role of women, is sympathetic to them, for he is himself, ultimately, humane in his probing and searching, his doubting and tolerance, his exposure of hypocrisy and evil.

MICHAEL LONGLEY, SEAMUS DEANE, DEREK MAHON and EILÉAN NÍ CHUILLEANÁIN

After being a schoolteacher in Dublin, London and Belfast, **Michael Longley** (b 1939), was Director of Combined Arts in the Northern Irish Arts Council. His first volume of poetry, *No Continuing City* (1969), shows the influence of Mac-Neice. His classicism – he read classics at Trinity College, Dublin – has enabled him to deploy an exuberant eclecticism in dealing with past and present tradition, for tradition shapes his own sensibility. 'In Memoriam' celebrates his father, wounded in the First World War, expanding into an elegaic feeling for those who suffer in war. This is a theme continued in 'Wounds', a poem in *An Exploded View* (1973), which moves from the First World War to the victims of contemporary violence in Northern Ireland.

In this volume, however, Longley casts a reflective, indeed a reductive, irony on his own poetic performance and the potential of various options. His third book, *Man Dying on a Wall* (1976), is less self-conscious and more effective, because he records details of the countryside in Co Mayo with an engaging simplicity, an accuracy which gives the impression of careful scientific observation.

In recording reactions to the horrors of contemporary violence in Northern Ireland, the poems of *The Echo Gate* (1979) manage to maintain a sense of historical perspective, the comments of 'Peace' reaching back into Roman times. In *Gorse Fires* (1991) Longley continues to use Carrigskeewaun as a setting for the details of Mayo life which he embraces with delight. In this volume, poems about his father see him in a role like that of Laertes, the father of Odysseus, and this permits emotional feeling to emerge far more freely, Longley blending translations from the *Odyssey* with his own lines. His preoccupation with war continues (there are times when it seems that, like the English poet Geoffrey Hill, he had been cheated of the chance of being a war poet by being born when he was). Longley is an assured poet whose autobiography *Tuppeny Sting* was published in 1994.

It would be logical to progress here chronologically to the poems of **Seamus Heaney** (b 1939), but instead it seems attractive to round off consideration of contemporary poetry with a discussion of his work, for the Nobel Prize winner is still developing, still actively creative and an apt figure with whom to conclude this book.

Seamus Deane (b 1940) has produced two volumes of poems, *Gradual Wars* (1972) and *History Lessons* (1983) which relate closely to the historical and sectarian situation in Northern Ireland. General editor of the *Field Day Anthology of Irish Literature* (1991), he has written various critical books as well as a novel *Reading in the Dark* (1996), short-listed for the Booker Prize in 1996.

Like Michael Longley a classicist by education – they were both at the Royal Belfast Academical Institution and then at Trinity College, Dublin – **Derek Mahon** (b 1941) has had an impressive career as a literary journalist; his adaptations for radio and television are, like his translations, very able indeed. He writes wry poetry of a detached kind, often relying upon personae or masks as a means of viewing the world with a degree of objectivity.

His first volume, *Night Crossing* (1986), emphasises wandering, 'Legacies' and 'An Unborn Child' its most memorable poems. In *Lives* (1972) he rejects archaeological links with the past as a means of exploring the present (an opposite view to that of Seamus Heaney). He takes a post-cataclysmic view of the world, which alters somewhat in *The Snow Party* (1975) where 'A Disused Shed in Co Wexford' is outside history: history is one extreme; there is also a desire to live, the shed a place for new life to begin. *Courtyards in Delft* (1981) continues his deepening meditative strain; still a bleak view but tempered somewhat by a grim wit. The title poem emphasises Mahon's belief in the relationship of art (written as well as painted) to human life. He can be Audenesque in some poems such as 'Beyond Howth Head' or 'The Sea in Winter' where he writes informally and decidedly irreverently. He can at times be unduly obscure in his allusiveness which leads to some unevenness in tone. The examination of an individual in a cold cosmos continues in *Antarctica* (1985). Mahon's *Selected Poems* were published in 1993; the volume confirms his technical accomplishment and his variety – from Kosangas to Kafka - of approach.

Eiléan ní Chuilleanáin (b 1942), educated at University College, Cork and Oxford, has an ability to deal with everyday description while providing unexpected insights, notably into classical subject matter. Her work includes *Art and Monuments* (1972), *Site of Ambush* (1975), *The Rose Geranium* (1981), probably her best work, and *The Magdalene German* (1990). She has a gift for accurate and effective translation well-demonstrated in her version of Pierce Ferriter's 'Lay Your Weapons Down'.

PAUL DURCAN

Of recent poets **Paul Durcan** (b 1944), educated at University College, Cork, whose first personal volume *O Westport in the Light of Asia Minor* appeared in 1975, arrests attention because of his highly inventive individual voice. Ironically irreverent about Church and State, he seems a measuring rod with which to plumb the emptiness left in old-style nationalism, the drop in the level from 1916-style idealism to the muddy pragmatics of present-day politics and religion. He writes in a colloquial manner, blithely undercutting as he goes.

'The Girl with the Keys to Pearse's Cottage' is a good example of how his irony works, contrasting the realities of de Valera's Ireland with that romantic past associated with Pearse. And he confronts the image of de Valera, President of Ireland (1957-1973), directly in 'Making Love outside Áras an Uachtaráin' (the presidential residence in Phoenix Park, Dublin).

His 'The Great Hunger' gives present-day social climbers and *nouveaux riches* Swiftian treatment, as does 'Anglo--Irish Agreement, 1986' with its picture of suburban Dublin's burglar alarms, poems included in his *Going Home to Russia* (1987).

Some of the bizarre titles in this book – 'Cardinal Dies of Heart Attack in Dublin Brothel' and 'Priest Accused of Not Wearing Condom' – resemble newspaper headlines and convey a disillusion with the Catholic church in terms which would have been unthinkable if published but a few years before. Such titles and images can be briefly amusing but they seem designed to disturb, even to destroy. Yet Durcan can appreciate: he is not all anger, weakness, error; he can pay tribute generously enough to other artists, notably in *Daddy Daddy* (1990), which won him the Whitbread Prize.

A new development in his work, apart from its increasing awareness of feminism, is the writing of two recent volumes *Crazy about Women* (1991) and *Give Me Your Hand* (1994) which are related, respectively, to paintings in the National Gallery of Ireland and the National Gallery, London.

Durcan's own highly-successful readings of his poems are crammed with intensity. His poems with their often grotesque, surrealistic attitudes are designed to impress readers and hearers with their continuous overflowing outrageousness, which, generally speaking, they do.

EAVAN BOLAND and OTHERS

The poems of **Eavan Boland** (b 1945) are written from a self-consciously feminine, often deliberately feminist, point of view. They explore the possibility of creating a new woman's pastoral; she thinks that women are deprived without their own cultural rituals, that there is an alienation from cultural roots in modern Irish urban society. Her first volume, *New Territory* (1967), contained skilful translations which show her deep awareness of past tradition. After writing *W B Yeats and His World* (1971) with Micheal MacLiammóir she began to speak in her own distinctive voice of the present time which is often so lacking in links with traditional culture.

The War Horse (1975) was followed by *Her Own Image* (1980) the poems of which face the problems of contemporary women in a society dominated by male stereotypes of a decidedly unpleasant if not always credible kind. Here, then, a frank emphasis is placed upon the physiological (such previously taboo-in-print-outside-women's-journals words as masturbation and menstruation), upon time's physical effects and the terror that realising their encroachment creates. 'Mastectomy' is typical of these dark poems, so resentful of men.

The title poem of *Night Feed* (1982), however, accepts, interprets and indeed celebrates details and even threatening elements of domestic life, somewhat to a reader's relief in reading chronologically through Eavan Boland's poems, for they pave the way for the cheerful liberalisingly joyful poems of *Outside History* (1990). *In a Time of Violence* (1994) emphasises the value of work and of domesticity, too, as a counterforce to the savagery sketched earlier in *The War Horse*, though a poem such as 'Ready for Flight' in that volume has moments of tenderness and acceptance:

And if a runner starts to run to me
Dispatched by you, crying that all is trampled
Underfoot, terraces smashed, the entry
Into holy places rudely sampled,

Then I would come at once my love with love

Bringing to wasted areas the sight
Of butterfly and swan and turtle dove
Their wings ruffled like sails ready for flight

In such surroundings, after the decease
Of devils, you and I would live in peace.

Like her carefully considered and cogently argued essays in
Selected Prose (1994) Eavan Boland's poems, at times ruthless
and savage, have to be seen as a steadily developing *oeuvre*
based upon an exacting sense of poetic technique.

Micheál Ó Siadhail (b 1947) a distinguished linguist
who was educated at Trinity College, Dublin, where he
taught before joining the staff of the Dublin Institute of
Advanced Studies, has published several collections of
poetry, including *Hail! Madam Jazz* (1992). *A Fragile City*
(1995) contains some sensitive love poems and poems
such as 'Celebration' which are unashamedly tender. His
poems are skilfully written and like many of those written
by his contemporaries deal with the changing events of
daily life with understanding.

Ó Siadhail's contemporary, **Hugh Maxton** (pseudonym
of **W J McCormack**, b 1947), is primarily a literary critic,
the author of, among other studies, *Sheridan Le Fanu and
Victorian Ireland* (1980) and *Ascendancy and Tradition in
Anglo-Irish History, 1789-1939* (1985). He has also several
collections of austerely intellectual poems to his credit,
among them *The Noise of the Fields* (1976), *At the Protestant
Museum* (1985) and *The Engraved Passion: New and
Selected Poems* (1992).

Frank Ormsby (b 1947) edited *The Honest Ulsterman*
for twenty years, and collected an *Amanda McKittrick Ros
Reader* (1988). (She wrote sentimental romances, *Irene
Iddesley* (1897) and *Delina Delaney* (1898), as well as vitu-
perative poems, and is a unique source of unintended

amusement for the enthusiast.) His own poems, preoccupied with details of daily life, are best encountered in *A Northern Spring* (1988).

Ciaran Carson (b 1948), Irish-speaking as a child, has been influenced by traditional music and storytelling, and some of his poems encapsulate the changing nature of 'the dark city of Belfast'. He allows his ideas freedom to wander amid complex syntax in *The Irish for No* (1987) and *Belfast Confetti* (1989), the storyteller's technique apparent in different versions of events. He enjoys the collecting of fragments and delights in cartoon-strip techniques, in digressions, in anecdotes.

Medbh McGuckian (b 1950), has been a schoolteacher and a writer in residence at her former university. She uses language elliptically, concentratedly, like the 'traplight' of 'Venus and the Sun'. She is interested in places and names of places, in rootedness, and in the different cultures of male and female. So her poems explore domestic situations; she uses images of growth and plantation; she refers back to her own body. 'To a Young Matron' is symptomatic of this; she is a poet who lays down layers of meaning in her poems as she explores differences between emotion and reality. *On Ballycastle Beach* (1988) and *Marconi's Cottage* (1991) demonstrate her growing involvement with European writers, her involvement with motherhood. At her best, she writes poems of a magnificent simplicity such as 'Branches' where she is detached from 'the fabric' that claims her.

NUALA NÍ DHOMHNAILL and PAUL MULDOON

Nuala ní Dhomhnaill (1952), educated at University College, Cork, writes poems in Irish which are vigorous, earthy, challenging and irradiated by a lively imagination;

they have been translated in *Rogha Dánta* (1988) by Michael
Hartnett, in *Pharoah's Daughter* (1991) by Ciaran Carson,
Seamus Heaney, Michael Longley and Paul Muldoon, and in
The Astrakhan Cloak by Paul Durcan and herself.

Paul Muldoon (b 1955), born in Co Armagh and
brought up in Co Tyrone, was educated at Queen's University, Belfast. He has a Joycean capacity for letting words
have their head, free association producing the arresting,
the unexpected. So he is witty, punning and homophoning
away in hermetic, anti-dogmatic, inconclusive style to considerable effect. *New Weather* (1973) has its 'mask lyrics',
outward signs for inner feeling, *Mules* (1977) its insistence
upon dividedness, an Ulster heritage, achieved by oppos-
ing idioms. (In his use of idioms Muldoon has been influenced by Louis MacNeice.) He packs several idioms into
one phrase and can cause confusion by changing tenses in
a poem: at times this can seem a coded, telegram style.

MacNeice had thought the character of the Irish could be
expressed as a set of antinomies; these, if rightly treated,
become assets. Muldoon takes these ideas further in *Why
Brownlee Left* (1980) and *Quoof* (1983, the word was used
by Muldoon's family for a hot water bottle). As 'Lunch with
Pancho Villa' puts it:

> For there's no such book, so far as I know
> As *How it Happened Here*,
> Though there may be. There may.

Quoof's poem 'The More a Man Has the More a Man Wants'
is perhaps the best example of his cumulative contradictory
style, while 'Immram', the last long poem in *Why Brownlee
Left*, is related to an Irish genre, the 9th century 'Immram
Maile Duin'.

Meeting the British (1987) continues Muldoon's sometimes self-indulgent exhibition of poetic techniques, his

habit of half-saying something which some writers argue may have been derived from Old Irish poetry. This volume, however, contains 'The Fox', a crisply direct and extremely effective poem.

In *Madoc* (1990) Muldoon has used as a framework Shelley's epic *Madoc* (linked with the youthful pantisocratic plan to establish a commune in New England on the banks of the Susquehanna) for his long poem with its sections associated, sometimes very tenuously, with major Western philosophers. The length of this eclectic, extensive, expansive poem may reflect the influence of American poets and the effect of enthusiastic critical reception of his poems, particularly in America, where he now lives.

SEAMUS HEANEY

The latest Irish Nobel Prize winner, **Seamus Heaney** (b 1939), was born and grew up in a small farm in Co Derry. A graduate of Queen's University, Belfast, where he was a lecturer from 1966 to 1972, he has since taught at Carysfort College in Dublin before becoming a Professor at Harvard in 1984. He spends some time there each year, some in Dublin and some at Glanmore, Co Wicklow. He has also been Professor of Poetry at Oxford. Heaney published his first volume of poems, *Death of a Naturalist* in 1966. These relate to his childhood sense of rural continuity as well as celebrating creativity. The images of the key opening poem 'Digging' recur through the volume. *Door into the Dark* (1969) with its closing poem 'Bogland' emphasises the myth of the bog as sanction for digging downwards through layers of accreted memory and emotional experience: 'The wet centre is bottomless'.

Wintering Out (1972) develops this image, especially in 'Tollund Man' which uses the victim of a ritual murder (found in a bog in Jutland and probably killed to bring about a good harvest) to offer a comment on Irish parallels, especially the present problems of the North. Heaney has refused to be drawn into over-direct comment upon the Ulster crisis: 'What we have', he has written in *Preoccupations* (1980), 'is the tail end of a struggle in a province between territorial piety and imperial power'.

He has portrayed Ireland as caught in the repetition of dark cults, of reciprocated outrages, of the pursuit of power in the poems of *North* (1975) where the victim in 'Bog Queen', 'Punishment' and 'Strange Fruit' is now a woman through whom he explores violence and revenge. He also continues his depiction of the details of life at Mossbawn, his family's farm, but echoes Yeats's Civil War poems in *Funeral Rites*:

> Now as news comes in
> of each neighbourly murder
> we pine for ceremony
> customary rhythms.

These are haunting, truly atmospheric poems. The note of experience runs through 'The Ministry of Fear' and 'A Constable Calls': 'And whatever you say, you say nothing'.

With *Field Work* (1979) Heaney reached a new level of skill. Again there is an echo of Yeats in 'After a Killing'. But while 'The Toome Road' has its own powerful, positive sense of belonging to the scene (rights of way, cattle, tractors, silos, gates, outhouses), there is a predominantly elegaic note in these poems. 'Casualty' is a good example of emotional reaction with its:

> After they shot dead
> The thirteen men in Derry.
> PARAS THIRTEEN, the walls said,
> BOGSIDE NIL.

There is then some relief, an emergence from such tensions into the good life of merely crossing a field in Ashford, Co Wicklow, in 'The Glanmore Sonnets', named after Glanmore Cottage, where Heaney came to live in 1972.

Sweeney Astray (1983), is a translation of *Buile Shuibne, The Frenzy of Sweeney*, a medieval Irish text dealing with King Sweeney's being driven mad by the sound of battle (as a result of a curse laid on him by a cleric) then wandering wild, in a naked or near-naked state, moaning over his fate and celebrating nature. Sweeney appeared again in the third part of *Station Island* (1984), the title poem set at St Patrick's Purgatory in Lough Derg, the site of a religious pilgrimage since early Christian days in Ireland. This pilgrimage has been used as a subject by many earlier writers. Heaney treats it as an opportunity to commune with the imagined ghosts – Carleton, James Joyce and Heaney's murdered cousin Colum McCartney, whose death at the hands of terrorists is the subject of *Field Work*'s 'The Strand at Lough Beg'. Carleton advises the poet to try to make sense of what comes; his cousin ignores his plea for forgiveness, for his 'timid circumspect involvement' ('Forgive my eye' he said), and later indirectly accuses him, who 'saccharined my death with morning dew'. The persona Sweeney Redivivus is alone, at home, 'in the camaraderie of rookeries', the worth of his 'First Kingdom' queried in the reductive poem of that name, paralleled by 'The Scribes', to whom he has never warmed.

The Haw Lantern (1987) is a series of interrogatory poems; Heaney questioning himself, the art of writing poetry, of writing itself. The poems begin with 'Alphabets', tracing the process of learning to fit shape and sound, seeing as well as saying, together. 'From the Frontier of Writing' moves from the troops inspecting a car on the way to the frontier of writing 'where it happens again'. The key poem in this volume, however, is 'From the Republic of Conscience'. When the poet lands there:

> it was noiseless when the engines stopped
> I could hear a curlew high above the runway

We have here a political picture going beyond Ulster into European situations where language used carefully (something he has always achieved) can help to overcome over-passive resignation to tyranny, as in 'From the Canton of Experience', 'The Mud Vision', a subtle poem which draws a line between panic and formulae, and 'The Disappearing Island' with its affirmation of achieving vision through loss.

Seeing Things (1991) continues to draw detail deftly – 'The Pitch Fork' will entrance anyone who has ever handled a pitchfork, tossing hay up into a barn, sweating and aware of the shaft's dark-flecked ash 'grown satiny from its own natural polish'. There is, of course, more to these poems than scrupulous observation and recording; though he is securing 'the bastion of sensation' Heaney is displaying his capacity to convey meaning of a deeper kind. He is more confident now, and with reason:

> Me waiting until I was nearly fifty
> To credit marvel.

Here again are echoes of Yeats's brief experience of great happiness in 'Vacillation', his fiftieth year come and gone, his feeling that he 'was blessèd and could bless'. The poem ends:

> So long for air to brighten
> Time to be dazzled and the heart to lighten

In the sequence of *Glanmore Revisited*, 'The Skylight' is in the same vein: the light is let in with miraculous effect when

the slates come off. The whole volume with its 'shifting bril-
liancies' creates an impression of light, indeed one section
is called 'Lightenings', and *xviii* of that section with its play
on light is characteristic of a personal optimism: 'when light
breaks over me', he thinks, he will be 'in step with what
escaped me'.

The Spirit Level (1996) has an insouciant freedom, a
self-confident, conversational, reminiscing ease about its
poems, incidents now recalled in a pleasing, self-
indulgent way, a clever use of sayings, or clichés, given a
deft twist, (as in 'Weighing In'). This is Heaney the world
traveller in relaxed mood; the friend, the family man, the
well-read man remembering his dead, his father treated
with the awe of true affection; this is the poet secure
enough to trust us, too, with his deep concern for the veri-
ties of love and living.

THE O'BRIEN POCKET SERIES

This series provides short but highly informative accounts of many aspects of Irish history, culture and politics, ideal for those seeking an insightful overview. Written by experts in each field, from academic and journalistic backgrounds, the series is renowned for its ability to provide worthwhile information, insight and understanding in easily absorbed text.

O'BRIEN POCKET HISTORY OF IRELAND
Breandán Ó hEithir

An overview of Ireland's history from earliest times to the late twentieth century.

Breandán Ó hEithir was a renowned journalist who provided sharp and witty comment on many aspects of Irish culture and Irish life. He was the author of several books.

O'BRIEN POCKET HISTORY OF GAELIC SPORT
Eamonn Sweeney

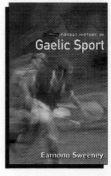

The thrill and excitement of Gaelic games, including hurling, football, camogie, handball, explored from their origins to the championships, players and great games of recent years.

Eamonn Sweeney has written several books on Gaelic sport, including *Munster Hurling Legends*, and contributes frequently to radio discussions and newspaper coverage of the games.

O'BRIEN POCKET HISTORY OF IRISH REBELS
Morgan Llywelyn

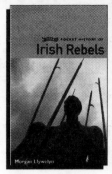

This books tells the stories and deeds of famous Irish rebels, including Granuaile, Owen Roe O'Neill, Wolfe Tone, Emmet, Daniel O'Connell, James Connolly, Markievicz, Pearse, Michael Collins, Bobby Sands ... and many more.

Morgan Llywelyn is an internationally renowned author of many books on Irish historical topics.

O'BRIEN POCKET HISTORY OF THE IRA
Brendan O'Brien

The story of the IRA from its foundation to today tracing the changes and developments that have influenced the organisation and the varying political environments in which it has operated.

Brendan O'Brien is one of Ireland's best-known investigative journalists and has covered the Northern Ireland situation for thirty years.

A POCKET HISTORY OF ULSTER
Brian Barton

Traces the background and unravels the historical complications of the Northern Irish state.

Brian Barton, historian at Queen's University Belfast, is the author of many historical works on Ulster.

O'BRIEN POCKET HISTORY OF THE TROUBLES
Brian Feeney

The most insightful short account of the complex story of Northern Ireland and the 'Troubles' of the past thirty years, from the early days of the Civil Rights Movement to the Assembly elections.

Brian Feeney, historian and commentator, has personal experience of the 'Troubles' and the politics of resolution. He is also author of the major historical book *Sinn Féin*.

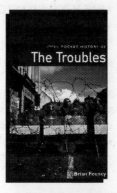

A POCKET HISTORY OF GAELIC CULTURE
Alan Titley

An entertaining and quirky account of Gaelic culture – its relationship with the Irish language in history, politics, music, dance, and games.

Alan Titley is a lecturer in Irish at St Patrick's College, Drumcondra, Dublin, and commentator on all matters related to Irish language and culture.

O'BRIEN POCKET HISTORY OF IRISH SAINTS
Brian Lacey

A concise history of over a hundred of the best-known and most influential saints and the wealth of folklore, legend, tradition and literature associated with them.

Brian Lacey is an archaeologist and former director of the Discovery Ireland programme. He has also written *Discover Derry*.

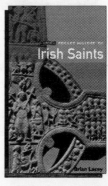

O'BRIEN POCKET HISTORY OF IRISH TRADITIONAL MUSIC

Gearóid Ó hAllmhuráin

The history of traditional music, song and dance from the mythological harp of the Dagda right up to Riverdance. Utilising a wide spectrum of historical sources it also traces the music of the Irish diaspora.

Gearóid Ó hAllmhuráin is a lecturer at San Francisco university, All Ireland concertina champion and historian and anthropologist.

**Send for our full-colour catalogue
or check our website**